25,00/18.75

UNIVERSITY WISDOM

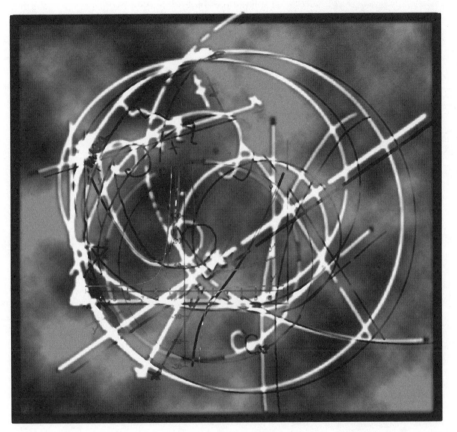

D1402182

ZERMATT PRESS
www.zermattpress.com

First Edition

Vanessa McCallum

Written by: Vanessa McCallum

Illustrated by: Alexandra Brooke
www.belleartiste.com

First Edition Published in 2006 by: Zermatt Press
www.zermattpress.com

Layout & Design by: S Graphics
www.sgraphics.com.au

Printed and bound in Australia

National Library of Australia Cataloguing-in-Publication entry

McCallum, Vanessa, 1971-.

University wisdom : discover the secrets of getting the most from your experience at university and use them as stepping-stones to launch your life and career - a practical guide for all students.

Bibliography.
Includes index.
For secondary students.
ISBN 13: 978 0 9775080 2 0 (soft cover).
ISBN 10: 0 9775080 2 1 (soft cover).
ISBN 0 9775080 0 5 (pdf.).
ISBN 0 9775080 1 3 (CD.).

1. Education, Higher - Australia.
2. Universities and colleges – Australia.
3. College students - Australia.
I. Brooke, Alexandra, 1975- .
II. Title. (Series : Practical wisdom ; 1).

378.94

IMPORTANT INFORMATION:

This book has been prepared without considering your personal objectives, financial position or needs.

Before acting on anything written here, you should consider its relevance to your situation.

Keep in mind that each person is responsible for their own decisions and actions.

Preface

The transition from High School to University is one of the more significant milestones faced by young people. The large, much less personal and often intimidating environment of the University replaces the personal and secure environment of the High School. Less emphasis is placed on teacher-directed learning and more onuses are placed on students to be responsible for their own learning.

Comfortable peer group relations are disturbed and, for many, the challenges of living away from home and managing personal finances are faced for the first time. Young people experience new temptations and questions relating to motivation, direction and meaning often arise for the first time. Is it any wonder that this time often causes students much anxiety and that not all navigate the difficulties without mishap?

Schools and Universities now invest considerable resources to help students manage their passage between High School and University. But given the individual nature of the issues confronted, ultimately the individual student must arrive at his or her own resolution. This book will be an invaluable guide. It is filled with good sense. Moreover, it is written in an accessible style and is full of interest.

The combination of well-written pithy advice, personal anecdotes, quotations, homespun philosophy and exercises for the readers to help refine their own thoughts, provides a medley of mutually reinforcing inputs which will ensure that the messages are transmitted effectively and retained. All the important topics are covered, including study skills, examination techniques, work-life balance, motivation, career choice, curriculum vitae preparation and many other areas. Vanessa McCallum has used the insight gained from her own experience, the experiences of her friends and family as well as her many years as a tutor at University in the preparation of this wonderful guide.

The transition to, and time spent at University cannot be considered in isolation from the rest of our lives and careers. Matters such as the decision to go to University, the choice of course and preparation for careers and lives beyond University are all dealt with in an interesting and informative way. Moreover, the emphasis in all these matters is on a rounded experience rather than a single focus on material or professional success. Participation in sporting activity and clubs and societies is encouraged.

Advice is individualized so that different assessments of what is important are accommodated with the over arching theme, as Einstein put it "We have to do the best we can. This is our sacred human responsibility". The goal-orientated, plan-driven nature of the advice given would delight Einstein! But it is leavened by a sympathetic tone, which provides a supportive framework for those who are less effective than the author in structuring and framing their lives and relentlessly ticking off achievements on their master plan of life.

Lives evolve in different ways, but the advice in this book will guide young people to a well rounded, rewarding University experience and prepare them for a rich and enjoyable life beyond University.

Richard G. Larkins

Richard Larkins AO
Vice-Chancellor and President, Monash University

Acknowledgements

I have many people to thank for helping me produce University Wisdom.

University Wisdom would not have been started but for the challenge put down by my good friend Anthony Fernando. He has helped me greatly with his encouragement as well as focusing my attention on High School graduates considering University.

Alexandra Brooke has creatively illustrated University Wisdom. Her intent was to keep the characters simple and fun, while portraying the underlying message of the book in a clear manner. I believe Alexandra has done a wonderful job.

University Wisdom would not have been finished but for the patience and support of my husband Rob. He brought me countless cups of tea while I wrote and rewrote chapters at all hours of the night.

Steve Guest from S Graphics has done a thoroughly professional job laying out this book and what's more, has been a pleasure to work with. Thanks for all the laughs Steve and for putting in such a big effort.

My proofreaders deserve a big "thank you" too, as they have helped me get my draft copy of University Wisdom up to a standard that is acceptable for a published book. Thank you to Mum and Dad, Rob, Angela Harrop, Anthony Fernando, Alan Kemp, Rosemary Peddie, Rosemary Sewell, Jess Denehey, Ross Wilmoth, Steve & Bev Guest, and Kathryn Smith.

Finally, I'd like to thank all the students I have tutored in the past, who asked the questions I have tried to answer in University Wisdom. Without this input, I would not have realised how important this information was to you all. Thank you for giving me the opportunity to write something useful for your generation and for the many students who will come after you.

This book is dedicated to my children Amelia and William.

Contents

PART 1

Where are you now?

Congratulations

Congratulations on deciding to do a course at University. You are embarking on a journey many people only dream of. Did you know that currently only around 1% of the worlds population get that opportunity?[1,2]

Try to appreciate how far you have come with your education and be proud to accept that you are now able to go on to University. It is a great achievement and you should celebrate the position you are in.

Now consider the people who have helped you get there. Think about your parents, friends, teachers and tutors, who have guided you in various ways. They may have helped you choose a course, or encouraged you to focus along the way, helping you achieve your dream of going to University. *It is important for you to accept the contributions of others.*

Seeking and accepting help is one of the fundamental steps towards being successful. No one ever truly achieves their potential without the help of others.

Whoever you need to be thankful to, stop and do it now. Give them a call, email them, write them a letter or just mention it next time you see them. This acknowledgement is very important for both you and them. It will help reinforce the idea that you are undertaking something very valuable.

Cherish the opportunity you have. You were not born with a ticket to University – you have earned the chance to go with a lot of hard work and determination and you have a team of dedicated helpers around you.

Being honest and accepting your limitations comes with maturity and some students just aren't ready for that before they go to University. This book is all about digging deep and finding real answers to fundamental questions. You will need to be totally honest with yourself if you are going to get any benefit from reading University Wisdom.

A University degree is not an essential ingredient for success. If you are not accepted into the course or University of your choice, all is not lost. Some of the greatest success stories I have read started that way. There are a multitude of courses available, with numerous campuses and institutions. There are also many careers that don't require a Higher Education at all.

Many people choose careers not even associated with the degree they gained at University. As life goes on, your ideas change and what is important to you now, may not be so important in a few years time.

Think of your degree at University as a stepping-stone to your career.

Your University degree will be a step from where you are now, to somewhere as a professional. You will be capable of advanced analysis, being employed in a professional environment, managing a company, doing research or starting a business. They are all very marketable qualities and ones that could lead you to different parts of the world, or give you a choice of a host of different careers.

The course you study at University or the campus you attend are just as important as your University 'experience'. The lessons you learn about life and the techniques you gain to help you in your chosen career are all factors that will shape the person you become as you enter the world after University.

Start your course with as much positive attitude as you can muster. Most courses are at least a year and some take up to six and seven years to complete. You will have some great times as well as some very average times. Occasionally, you may wonder why you ever started the course in the first place, so it is important for you to prepare for and learn how to manage these shifts in motivation.

It's those times, when you feel like giving up, that you should remember how fortunate you are to be part of the 1% of people throughout the world who get the opportunity to study at University. Most people don't have the choices you have. Again, cherish those who have helped you and value how far you have already come before you think of giving up the opportunity. In most cases, the chance you have now may not resurface for a very long time, if at all.

Like any other, this book cannot guarantee you success at University. For a start, your success is totally up to how you define it, and what steps you take to reach it. Your success is not necessarily measured by what subjects you take, nor the marks you receive. By the time you finish University Wisdom, you may find that it doesn't matter what job you get at the end of your course; your success is better judged by what you *do* with your knowledge and your view of the world after experiencing further education.

University Wisdom will also help you learn about yourself. It is important to not only read the text but also do the exercises. You may learn some knowledge about how to become successful without the exercises but remember that knowledge is quickly forgotten if it is not put into practice. By taking the time to write answers in the spaces provided, you will think about the questions more seriously and take responsibility for your answers. Even if no one else but you reads the answers, the exercises may be of great benefit to you now and in the future.

Summary

- Acknowledge the hard work you have done to get you where you are now
- Be grateful to all the people who have helped you along the way
- Think of your degree at University as a stepping-stone to your career

What is University?

The Oxford Dictionary of Current English describes the word 'University' as an 'educational institution instructing or examining students in many branches of advanced learning, and conferring degrees.' If you are about to begin learning at an institution after you finish High School, then as far as the context of this book is concerned, you are going to University! I am making this generalisation because the term University is not important – the fact that you are learning after you leave High School is.

The word University has many different meanings around the world, so I won't get technical and say that this book was written for students attending some institutions and not others. I would rather be more general and say that this book has been written for students attending any institution offering post High School education: this includes Colleges, TAFEs, Polytechnics and Institutions for any type of further adult education. It would also be useful for students attending Universities remotely over the Internet.

University Wisdom also includes practical tips for any adult who is willing to take on post High School education. Although most first year University students have come straight from High School, there are a number of adults who go to University for the first time after being out of school for many years. They may be studying on a full-time or part-time basis depending on their work or family commitments.

Whether you'd like to study for your first degree, change the job you're in, get a better salary, start your own business or just discover something new, University Wisdom can help expand your mind, allowing your skill set for success to become more complete.

Like everyone else, I had some really low times at University and I also saw some of my peers go through hardship too. *I would like to encourage you, as a student, to follow your dream and do whatever it takes to become the person you want to be.*

Although the decision to go to University is a tough one, once you decide to go, you have to be prepared for many challenges. University life won't be easy. There will be some sort of challenge that stretches you every day. University Wisdom can help you with the mental preparation you need to succeed, as well as the methods to get you through the course efficiently.

> **"If you can find a path with no obstacles, it probably doesn't lead anywhere."** Frank A. Clark

This book is not about any specific course or University. Many of these ideas are relevant to any student, doing any course, anywhere in the world. It focuses on your mindset as you enter the world of a University student. It establishes how to fully utilise your opportunity. It is about succeeding not only with your course but your life during the time you are a student and well after graduation. It opens your mind to what you are learning and what is important about your University degree. You might be surprised at what is ultimately important and equally with what is not.

Summary

- *University is a place where people learn new skills*
- *There are many different courses and institutions around the world*
- *Obtaining a University degree is both challenging and rewarding*

Discover Your Influences

Every day we are influenced by the people we live and work with, what we see on the television and Internet, what we hear on the radio and what we read in the newspapers. It is important to understand and recognise what is influencing you to go to University and make your course choices.

If you know what your main influences are now, you can save yourself the trouble of blaming anyone later on, if things don't go to plan or you are not happy with your decisions. If, on the other hand, you have a positive experience at University and go on to do great things, you will be able to appreciate those who influenced your decision.

It is important to write out a list of who or what is influencing you so you understand your motivation for striving for a University qualification. This may be a challenging task, but it is an important one. It is better to think about it now and fully understand *why* you are making this decision.

My main thought(s) influencing my decision to go to University is/are

_____

_____

_____

The main person(s) influencing me to go to University is/are

_____

_____

_____

The main reason(s) I haven't been to University before is/are

_____

_____

_____

The benefits I will get later on from going to University are

_____

_____

_____

If I didn't get the marks I needed to get into the course of my choice I would

_____

_____

_____

The final decision for me to go to University was made by

_____

_____

_____

Other people I know who will be doing the same course as me are

_____

_____

_____

Once you understand the answers to all these questions, you will have a clearer picture of *why* you are about to go to University. It is important to ensure you are making this decision for your own reasons. If this exercise has revealed that you feel pressured to go to University by someone else and you really don't want to go, then it is important to sit down with this person and work through the issues.

A person's history is an excuse some people use to make themselves more comfortable about their achievements, or lack of them. Your history, or your family's history, has *nothing* to do with where you are going from this day forward. Your history or that of any member of your family neither guarantees your success nor prevents you from being successful.

"It doesn't matter who you are, or where you come from, the ability to do something is within you always"
Oprah Winfrey

Everyone has influences around them which have to be put into perspective. Advice is sometimes good and sometimes bad. Listening to advice is always good as it is a way to gather information. Sifting through the advice you receive is required to determine what you want to use and what you want to discard. What you actually *do* with the advice you want to use is where you will make leaps towards your own definition of success.

Having a positive attitude at the start of your course will make it much easier for you to adjust to your new lifestyle and increase the chances of a successful outcome. If you are happy about your decision to go and are comfortable with the course you have chosen then all you have left to do is the work. You will already be part of the way to the finish line, even before your first day on campus. *Know why you are going and be positive about your decision!*

Summary

- *Your decision to go to University should be clearly understood*
- *Take responsibility for your decision to go to University*
- *Having a positive attitude towards your course is the first step towards success*

Is University For You?

Challenges

Most students going to University have worked exceptionally hard to get there and are really happy to be going. There are some students however who go to University for the wrong reason or who have a negative attitude towards their course and tend to struggle from day one.

There will be a few who may have no interest in any further studies but go to University because they did well at High School and feel they 'should'. Some students never intend to use what they learn at University in their chosen career but complete a course anyway, feeling forced to go by family or other pressures. Others just fear the sense of failure if they don't go. These students tend to feel they are wasting their time, even before they start.

If any of these sound like you, don't give up immediately. Getting through any course at University is hard work and you will never use everything you learn during your course in your career.

If you are not completely sure you want to attend University or complete your chosen course, you have the following choices:

a)   You can take what seems to be the easiest choice and quit.

If you feel like quitting before you've even started, make sure you have something else you'd far rather be doing before you make any decision. You don't want to quit just because you *think* it might be too hard, or because someone else you know is quitting. Consider your alternatives. Just because you dislike the thought of a subject or the campus you are attending, don't think you have a good reason to quit. Any exciting job or business will also have elements in it that you don't like.

Try to understand that University is merely a stepping-stone to your career. You won't be there forever and in most cases, you are there purely to learn how to learn for yourself. If you have a really good reason why you don't want to go after being given the opportunity, you alone will have to be comfortable with your decision. Don't let the opportunity go lightly.

b)   You can try to work out what you don't like about University and go about changing it.

If you find that the work is hard, get yourself a tutor. If you are constantly tired, get more sleep and find a sport or hobby that restores your health and wellbeing. If you are just sick of being at school, plan to defer for a while. If your relationship with your partner is interfering with University life, explain the problem with the intent of finding a resolution, seek professional guidance or reassess the relationship.

You can never be everything to everyone and no one should ever expect you to be. Nor should you put so much pressure on yourself that you become unhappy. There is usually a solution to every problem students face at University and you will not be the first or only one to experience them. All you have to do is identify the problem and then go about finding a solution.

c)   You can accept that life at University is a unique experience and although difficult at times, allows you to grow while finding ways of overcoming each challenge as they arrive.

With this attitude, you can embrace the challenges of University and see your experience as a stepping-stone to almost anything you want to do.

Pressures

Some students become stressed if they are not at the top of their class. The perceived risk of not excelling can cause the problem to compound and many very bright students give up because of the pressure they put themselves under. Controlling this type of internal stress is highly recommended in order to successfully complete your course. It is better to complete a University degree and pass with average grades than to start a course and never finish it.

You may change your mind about your career half way through your course. Perhaps you'd rather go into business for yourself. Having a certain degree may not directly help you in your business, but the skills you learn at University are not just about content. Any course will teach you how to learn, how to research, how to speak in public, how to write reports, how to come to conclusions, how to network and many other important skills that will help you in a business.

Finances

If you don't want to go to University because you'd rather get out into the work force and 'earn lots of money', think about the long-term earning potential you may be giving up. Short-term financial rewards have caused many people a lot of heartache when they look back and realise that a bit of hardship and long-term thinking could have been a better investment financially and personally. Remember, many students work part-time to pay their way through University and there are many programs around that offer students financial help.

If you still think University is not for you, it may very well not be - it's not for everyone. There is no point struggling through 3 to 5 years of work if you know it will be a waste of time. You may have something else you desperately want to do. Just weigh up all your options and make your decision based on logical clear thinking, not solely emotion. Then go out and do what you choose to do, with all your energy!

For more information about the many career choices you have once you finish High School, go to:

www.year12whatnext.gov.au

Summary

- *Not everyone is convinced that they will enjoy University before they start*
- *There are always solutions to problems faced by students*
- *Try to control the amount of stress you place on yourself*

Define Success For You

Have you ever thought about what it would be like to be successful? What is your definition of success? Very few people spend time thinking about how they would define success for themselves. Without goals you can become bored and frustrated in life, as there is little to strive for. If you know what your definitions of success are, you can aim your life towards those goals and when and if you get there, you will have a much better chance of feeling fulfilled. Remember, journeys towards a goal can often turn into another goal with a different destination.

Success doesn't just arrive one day by mail in a single packet. Success can be broken down into at least five main areas: Educational, Financial, Family, Health and Freedom. It is important to strive in all areas, as they work together to make you successful in a balanced way. There is no point for instance being financially successful whilst at the same time, totally unhappy in life and lacking the freedom to do what you choose to do.

People's sets of success definitions can vary greatly - There are no right or wrong answers!

Educational success is very interesting. Some students going to University try to get their degree with the least amount of effort so they can get a job and start earning money. At the other end of the spectrum, students want to pass every subject with High Distinctions. They may strive to get a job with a 'top firm', or go on to further study. They aim to go as far as possible with their education because they value that more than the money a job could earn them.

What is your idea of educational success? Would you be happy if you passed your course and went out into the work force? Or would you strive for higher results, increasing your opportunities, or perhaps stay on at University to do more advanced courses? Briefly describe your definition of educational success.

My idea of educational success is:

_____

_____

_____

_____

Financial success is often a moving target, as people generally earn more as they get older and more experienced. As people earn more money, they generally spend more money and their ideas towards money and spending change. This is a definition that will develop over time, so it is worth reviewing it every few years.

There are some people who are happy to work for enough money to pay their bills and have a little extra for occasional luxuries. Others see financial success when they can live comfortably from passive income. Passive income is money generated without having to work for it. It can come from bank interest, rent from real estate, royalties from a book or computer program, or profits from a company for example. Living off passive income means you are never spending your capital and your money or your investments work for you.

What is your idea of financial success? Would you be happy to earn enough money to pay your bills and have occasional luxuries or would you rather earn enough passive income so that you don't have to work? Briefly describe your definition of financial success.

My idea of financial success is:

_____

_____

_____

_____

Family success relates to how you would like your relationships to unfold. Some people are quite happy to go from one relationship to another or avoid having a relationship at all. Others strive for a steady, long-term relationship that may result in marriage and having children. Some people struggle with their immediate family relationships (eg parents, brothers and sisters) while others work hard to make them positive.

What is your idea of family success? Would you be happy to go from relationship to relationship or are you looking for one that is long-term and has solid foundations? What about your immediate family relationships? Briefly describe your definition of family success.

My idea of family success is:

_____

_____

_____

_____

Health success is all about how well and fit you would like to be. Some people don't really think about their health. They eat what and when they like and don't get involved in any sport or activities at all. Diet-related disease is often a result of this kind of lifestyle. Others feed their body and mind good foods, plan their meals, exercise and enjoy a healthy lifestyle.

What is your idea of health success? Are you happy just eating for convenience and avoiding sports and activities or do you strive to stay healthy and fit? Briefly describe your definition of health success.

My idea of health success is:

_____

_____

_____

_____

Freedom success concerns your ability to do what you want to do. It is influenced by two of the most restrictive quantities in life, time and money. Freedom is not gained until you have both the money and the time to do exactly what you want to do. Some people are happy to be able to pursue a hobby on the weekend. Others strive to be able to give up their job so they can go out and develop an invention or donate their time to a charity. A freedom project is not something you would do to earn money to pay for bills – you only do it because you *want* to do it.

What is your idea of freedom? Would you be happy to pursue a hobby on the weekend and if so, which one would you choose? Perhaps freedom to you would be to have the time to spend with your family or to dedicate all your time to a charity. Perhaps you'd like to travel the world. Briefly describe your definition of freedom success.

My idea of freedom success is:

_____

_____

_____

_____

_____

Working towards your ideas of success will allow you to avoid the frustration of not really knowing what you want. When you become successful in one aspect of life, be happy! Then focus on the remaining areas until you are successful by your own definition in all areas. By updating your definitions regularly, you will be fine tuning your ideals and reinforcing them into your personality. In doing that, you will also be giving yourself the best chance of making them happen. Are there any other areas of your life that you would like to work on - such as your spirituality, or your inner peace?

Summary

- *Your success should only be determined by your own definitions*
- *There are at least five areas of success to strive for*
- *When you reach your own definitions of success – be happy!*

Where do you want to go?

PART 2

Choosing a Course

Career Suitability

When you think about having a job or running a business, what can you see yourself doing? Would you like to be indoors or outdoors, work in an office or be far away from the city? Would you like to work with people or are you happy not to? These questions should narrow down some of the vast choices you have when you are choosing a course to study at University.

Getting Advice

There are many people you can ask for career advice: people at your school, the local library, friends of your family or professionals in the work force. There are also many books written about careers and the types of courses available at Universities. An Internet search using the word 'career' or 'University course' would be a good start to finding information.

For Australian University courses, go to: **www.goingtouni.gov.au/CourseSearch.htm**

Work Experience

There should also be some opportunity for you to 'try out' a career during a work experience program while you are at school. If this is not available to you, try ringing a local business of interest to see if you can get experience on the weekends.

It's important that you enjoy and are suited to the everyday reality of your chosen career. There is no point idealising about a job or business, if the reality is totally different. This will only lead to disappointment. By trying out a career through work experience, you will very quickly determine your suitability to it.

The course you study at University does not 'lock you in' to that career for life.

There will undoubtedly be more than one career that will suit you, so try not to be totally 'one-eyed' when choosing a course. Keeping your options open will allow you to manoeuvre if you are not offered your first choice, or if you change your mind later on.

Personality Testing

There are many tests you can take to determine the sorts of jobs you would be suited to. These Psych or Personality tests provide employers with useful information about you when they try to fill job vacancies. They can also be useful tools for you when deciding which course to study at University. A common tool employers use is the Myers-Briggs® Type Indicator test.

> I was tested with the Myers-Briggs Type Indicator on numerous occasions at High School and University and each time I came up with the same result. I am an ISTJ type of person. That simply means that I have likes and dislikes in what I do and I react with people and groups in a certain way. From the description of what an ISTJ person is, it's no wonder I enjoy being an engineer.

There is a website providing a free, 4 question psych test at:

www.haleonline.com/psychtest/

This type of test may help you have a greater understanding of your own personality. The description of your personality type might give you some indication of what careers you may be suited to. It only takes a minute and is very interesting!

Eliminating unsuitable careers

There are some courses you think might be appealing until you realise there are aspects of the job or business that you would avoid or not enjoy at all. Using a process of elimination, you can narrow down a course list to a manageable number of choices. Here is a simplified version of a process of elimination to try to highlight a suitable career or University course.

Write down six careers or University courses you think you might be suited to.

1. _____ ☐   2. _____ ☐

3. _____ ☐   4. _____ ☐

5. _____ ☐   6. _____ ☐

Write down some aspects of a career or course you would *like* to do every day, such as 'work with people'.

_____

_____

If there are any careers or courses in the list above that *do not* include these aspects, then mark them with a cross in the box.

Write down some aspects of a career or course you would *not* like to do every day, such as ' work in an office'.

_____

_____

If there are any careers or courses in the list above that *do* include these aspects, then mark them with a cross in the box.

You should now have eliminated a few of the six careers or courses you originally chose. Use more descriptions of likes and dislikes until you are left with just one career or University course.

Write down the remaining career or University course. _____

Do some research into this career or course. Does it seem like a logical one to study?

There is a really useful website that expands this process more fully at: **www.myfuture.edu.au**

The results from this resource can then be discussed with your career advisor at school.

Summary

- *There may be many careers that you are suited to and would be happy in*
- *Your decision now is not going to 'lock you in' for life*
- *Get to know yourself, as it will help you in your course choice*

Plan For Success

Once you have chosen a course to study at University, your next goal should be to set up a strategy to successfully complete it. University can be one of the biggest challenges in life and a plan will greatly help your chances of holding a certificate at the end. Planning is a very simple and easy tool that doesn't take a lot of time or effort, yet the benefits of planning can be enormous.

Your ability to balance and plan your life could ultimately give you the skills you need to succeed way beyond your wildest dreams. These skills can help you in all aspects of your life. 'Planning to fail' and 'failing to plan' achieve the same outcome, so set a path towards your goals and follow it.

Planning requires goals to be written down with expected time frames. The magnitude of these goals and the time frames can only be set by you, as you will be responsible for delivering them. You also have to set *achievable* goals, so break down any that sound unattainable into smaller ones that follow a logical order.

"If you think you can, or you think you cannot, you are right"
Henry Ford

Only you can determine the level of the goals you set yourself and decide how much effort to put into each one. If you set your goals at the same level as everyone else, you will stay in an average position. If you truly want to achieve more, you will have to set your goals higher than the majority of other students.

Once you have set your plan in place, your greatest asset is the time you have to implement it. There is no point finding out how to be successful at the end of your life when you have all the time in the world to read books like this one. You won't have the time left to enjoy the fruits of your labour. What you can do now is work out where you want to go and put a plan in place to help make it happen.

Many people don't have a plan and drift through life being pushed and pulled around by their influences. They fall into the trap of thinking 'Life wasn't meant to be easy' and 'don't worry, it wasn't meant to be'. Taking charge of your direction by having a plan makes life a lot easier because what you need to do is right in front of you. It also gives you a sense of power to know you are in control of your own destination.

Read through each of the following sentences carefully and tick any that you have said or thought in the past or would say right now.

- [ ] I wish someone had told me that when I was younger.
- [ ] I wish I had someone who could guide me.
- [ ] Why didn't I read that book I was given?
- [ ] I wish I had done that when I was told about it. Now it's too late.
- [ ] I could do so much more if I could organise my time better.
- [ ] I know all that - I don't need to read about it.
- [ ] I don't have time to do any of that.
- [ ] I get jealous when other people succeed.
- [ ] Why would I want to plan my life? – that would be boring.

Don't let this passive attitude and lack of control become part of your later life regrets.

Now read each of the following sentences and put a tick against the ones you want to be able to say openly and honestly to your family and friends…

- ❏ I am so glad I found out about this.
- ❏ I have a plan now and I know where I'm going.
- ❏ I am excited about what I am going to learn.
- ❏ I know now that I can and will achieve my goals.
- ❏ When I reach my first goal I will _____
- ❏ Other people's success will only ever inspire me.
- ❏ I can't wait to get to University!

This type of attitude will help you achieve your goals and fulfil your plans.

A plan might only take you half an hour to do. It doesn't have to be long – a page should be enough to write down your long and short-term goals. Remember to keep your plan in a place where you will come across it often, like in your diary or up on a wall at home and review it regularly.

In the space below, jot down some ideas for your short-term plan. What do you hope to achieve before you go to University?

_____

_____

_____

_____

My long-term plan was stuck up on my bedroom wall while I was at University. It was hand written on a single piece of paper and it outlined what I wanted to achieve during the next five years. Because I saw it nearly every day, it was a constant reminder to me of what my focus was.

I had five things I wanted to achieve in those years. My plan read "Work in Switzerland, Go to Antarctica, Finish my degrees, Achieve the Life-Saving Distinction Award and Climb the Matterhorn. There is only one of those goals I am now yet to achieve but I know I will get to Antarctica one day.

My long-term plan is totally different now and includes some very exciting goals. By achieving your goals you open up new opportunities.

Summary

- *A plan is a list of goals with time frames*
- *Any large goal can be broken down into achievable steps*
- *Being organised with a plan makes it easier to achieve goals*

Be Inspired

Inspiration is a great motivating force when you set yourself a difficult goal. As humans, we like to take the easy options. When life starts to get tough, we often find excuses to quit. Being inspired allows you to overcome those natural tendencies because your sights are set on something very important to you. It allows your mind to focus on what is beyond the hardship you may be experiencing.

Athletes who win gold medals at Olympic games often dedicate their achievements to someone dear to them who has either died or become seriously ill. The emotions of life and love can inspire them to produce superhuman achievements. They can take emotional pain and turn it into sporting genius. Winners often say that an Olympic gold medal is 80% physical ability and 20% mental attitude. Being inspired gives you that attitude. It drives you to higher levels than you would ever think imaginable.

Elite athletes don't complain about the many thousands of times they have to practise a technique, even if it becomes boring and painful. They know that to be the best in the world at a sport, practise is just part of the required training. The thought of winning an Olympic gold medal is their inspiration. They look beyond the pain and see themselves on the podium with everyone cheering.

> The Matterhorn inspired me during my five years at University. In my first year, one of our lecturers told us that five students from my course would have the opportunity to go to Switzerland and work for six months after our fourth year. Within two seconds, I had decided that I was going to be one of them. The thought of going to work in a beautiful country while I was a student and be paid for the privilege gave me the determination to focus on my work and concentrate on making the five. The extra effort I found within myself meant that everything I did mattered. Nothing was done with an attitude of 'who cares' or 'I'm tired and couldn't be bothered'.
>
> The criteria to be chosen to go to Switzerland were not based on being at the top of the class. Attitude to the course and the ability to work with others was just as important.
>
> The trip to Switzerland for me was a goal that I focused on right through my first four years of the course. When I was told I had been chosen to go, I was thrilled and spent the next few months working overtime to get the money together for my flights. The experience I had with ABB (Asea Brown Boveri) was fantastic. They employed students from all over the world so we made many friends and spent most weekends skiing and travelling around Europe.

The Matterhorn, featured on the cover of this book, has for many years been one of my biggest inspirations. Climbing it was something I really wanted to do. Achieving that goal in 1994 is still one of the highlights of my life and I think back to that day with great memories. As I write *University Wisdom*, it gives me the inspiration to finish one more chapter. I would far rather be tucked up asleep in my bed but I know finishing this book is something I really want to achieve. Nothing worthwhile comes without hard work and dedication. Getting through a University course is no different.

Finding Your Inspiration

Do you have an inspiration? If you haven't, it's OK. You may not have thought about this before. You might have someone else who is trying to inspire you like a parent or a sports coach. Although their words of encouragement can lead you to do more than you would do otherwise, it's not the same as if you were driven by your own inspiration.

Your own inspiration will enable you to look at what you are doing in a totally different light and you will no longer wait for someone else to give you words of encouragement.

Think of one goal that, given the opportunity, you would give up every creature comfort to be able to achieve. This goal might be an experience of a lifetime, or a sporting achievement. It might be something that you have dreamed about but never thought would be possible in your lifetime. Write down your goal in the space below.

My goal is to _____

I am inspired by _____

Breaking your Goal down into Achievable Steps

Now think about all the things you will need to do in order to achieve that goal. Remember that often goals can take many years of hard work. So if it sounds unattainable now, don't just drop the idea. If your inspiration is strong enough and your goal is given enough thought you may be able to visualise yourself actually achieving it. If it gets under your skin and you work at it, you may just find a way of achieving it.

Visualising the Achievement of your Goal

A powerful way of cementing an inspiration into your mind is to regularly look at a picture of what it is you hope to achieve. Let's say, your goal is to be able to help some of the many people in Africa, using your skills as a doctor. That would be a fine and noble aspiration if you were contemplating studying for a medical degree. Now imagine yourself reading through a medical textbook with three assignments due the following week. You have a heavy work-load and you are tired. You know that you have to get through your text book before you can start the assignment but you would rather just go to bed. It would be tempting if you lacked an inspiration.

Now imagine this same scenario with one key difference. Right in front of you there is a picture of a doctor treating a sick African child and another one of the same child with a big happy smile after being treated. Don't you think staying up an extra hour to read the text would be easier if you had a picture of your inspiration in front of you? Of course it would. What you have to do in order to achieve your goal becomes insignificant compared to the goal itself. You appreciate the opportunity you have to achieve your goal and focus less on all the hoops you have to jump through in order to achieve it.

Visualisation is a very powerful tool. Find a picture that relates to your goal and what inspires you and put it up on a wall where you will see it every day.

Planning to Achieve your Goal

Write down what steps you will have to go through in order to achieve your goal. Remember, that if your goal was to help the African people using your skills as a doctor, then going to University to complete a medical degree is an important hurdle that you must get over. Other requirements might sound trivial, like getting the money together for an air fare, but they are just as necessary as the University degree if you are truly going to make it happen.

In order for me to _____

I will need to:

1) _____

2) _____

3) _____

4) _____

5) _____

6) _____

7) _____

8) _____

9) _____

10) _____

You may need help to achieve some of these requirements. Don't think that if you can't do it all on your own, then it's not worth doing. Any goal that you feel passionately about and you want to achieve is worth striving for. Most people who do great things have lots of help along the way. Elite athletes hire a coach and I hired a guide to take me up the Matterhorn. The achievement of fulfilling the goal is far more important than the hurdles put in front of you, or the help you receive along the way.

Figure 1: My inspiration was the Matterhorn throughout my University degree. Here I am on the summit with my guide Charni at 4,478m (14,693 feet) above sea level, 28 August 1994.

If you would like a little inspiration, go to www.universitywisdom.com/inspiration

Summary

● *An inspiration can help you focus on achieving your goals*

● *An inspiration that comes from within you is most powerful*

● *A visual reminder of your goal and inspiration will help cement it in your mind*

Think Beyond Your Marks

There have been many disturbing stories describing how some students have dealt with the pressures of not living up to either their own expectations or the expectations of family and friends regarding the marks they receive at High School or University. Some students have gone to the extreme of harming themselves and/or others because they could see no way out of what had become for them, an unbearable situation.

It is unfortunate that there has to be an objective system for Universities to sift through the many capable and wonderful students applying for courses each year. There has to be *some* way to determine who is granted a place and who is not. Think of the consequences if this did not happen. Universities would have more students than they could cope with attending one course or another and not enough attending others. As a society we would have more lawyers or economists for example than we needed and many newly qualified graduates would be unable to find suitable jobs in their field.

With the current system, if you do well at High School then it is most likely you'll get into a course of your first or second choice. The system seems fair, although it does favour those who have grasped the concepts of being organised and having good exam technique at the High School level.

When I was at High School I was flying through all my subjects, and was well on my way to becoming a vet. I found most Maths and Physics subjects a breeze and coped well with Chemistry and Biology. I struggled with English but I performed above average and generally had all my homework up to date.

When I had to sit a small test in Physics that counted for 3% of my overall mark, I went confidently into the classroom, as I had studied all the relevant work and had a good grasp of the subject. Everything we had done up to that point was considered practice exams and tests that didn't count towards our final mark. I walked into the class and sat down, looked at the paper and froze. My heart started pounding and I began to sweat. I knew straight away that I was going to stuff the whole thing up. I was very used to getting 90% and above for tests. Anything below that was unacceptable for me and it was me alone who set that standard.

As I sat there, my emotions started to run wild and I kept thinking about failing the test - something I hadn't done before. Everyone else was scratching away with their pens on paper and I hadn't written anything. I tried to find some numbers to begin with but every time I wrote something down, I couldn't see how it was going to help me.

The test was all about an experiment we had done in class that I had found very easy. Yet, I couldn't understand the questions and it took me ages to get started and find some reasonable answers. My best friend at the time was at the top of the Physics class and when she saw me after the test, she knew something was wrong. I didn't even want to talk to her about it. I wanted to curl up into a little ball and hide.

When I got home, I burst into floods of tears. My mum got me a cup of tea, put me into her bed and lay there holding me. I cried my heart out for probably over an hour. By that stage I was worn out and ready to start listening. Mum asked with a smile 'Is it really all that bad'? I told her how I had just thrown away 3% of my Physics score for the whole year and that I couldn't believe I had failed the test after all the study I had done. I told her that I wouldn't be able to get into Veterinary Science, which is what I had wanted to do since I was a child.

I sobbed and sniffed and carried on for a little while longer before mum said to me 'So what was the test actually worth'? I told her 3% of my school rated grade for Physics. Then she asked 'so what is the end of year exam worth'?

I said '90% of my overall Physics mark'. She thought about it for a while and added; 'So even if you get a zero for this test, which I'm sure you won't, you've only lost 3% of the 10% that your school grades you on'. I thought for a while. 'Yes, I suppose so' I said as I blew my nose. I could tell she was starting to calculate. 'So let's say you get zero for this test. Doesn't that mean that you could still get 99.7% for Physics if you get everything else right'? Her words slowly started to sink in. My anger with myself turned into embarrassment. 'Yes' I said, with a hint of a smile. I lay there kicking myself for being so stupid. I was amazed how worked up I had become over something so insignificant.

As I started to relax, mum told me how she thought this was a good thing and that I should learn from the experience. The lesson: If you work yourself up into a state over a test, a sports competition or anything else you place great importance on and you expect to do really well, get a perfect score or win the competition, you will often perform at a lower standard. If you go in well prepared, expecting to find questions that you may have trouble answering, have realistic expectations and a determination to do your best, then you are more likely to perform and feel better about your achievement.

For me, it was a turning point in my life. I was known as a 'mad scientist' by family and friends. People were surprised whenever they heard I had not received full marks. I used to beat myself up when I didn't get 100% because I thought I should have! I wasn't a nerd but I was probably heading down that track. When you are used to high marks and this happens, you can either take it out on yourself or friends and family as I did initially, (remember, I didn't want to talk to my best friend at the time) or, learn from it and listen to those prepared to help you with the wisdom of their experience.

My friend Rob, who later became my husband, did a bit of 'oohing and ahhing' to stir me up, before he said 'Ness, look on the bright side! You can't expect to just keep getting A's and it will be character building for you'. At the time, I didn't understand fully what he was talking about. I tried to hide my disappointment. But this experience was for me the opportunity to break away from the highly theoretical, 'perfect or nothing' sort of person I was to the more down to earth, practical and liveable person I am today. A little bit of pain and struggling doesn't hurt you - it's character building! I never let myself get worked up before an exam again.

I used this lesson while I was at University and I continue to use it today. At University, while I still worked very hard, my aim was not necessarily to get straight A's but to do my best and complete my course before anything else. I expect to make mistakes occasionally and when I do, I don't let them upset me like I used to. Rather I just try to learn from them.

Putting life into perspective is all the more important since the wake up calls of 9/11 and the latest tsunami disasters in Asia. If all you have to worry about are your marks, you are very lucky. If you ever find yourself getting stressed over the marks you obtain at University, try to put some perspective on them. Remind yourself how fortunate you are to be going to University at all and focus your energy on getting over the hurdles in front of you.

Summary

- *Avoid putting excessive pressure on yourself – keep your marks in perspective*
- *Talk to the people who care for you when you feel disappointed*
- *You can't change your mistakes so learn from them!*

Body Care

Caring for your body is an essential part of your success while studying at University because it will directly determine how you will function during the day. Your body will be put through some of the most taxing challenges imaginable. Sitting for hours writing essays or studying for exams, competing at University Games and reading texts for long periods of time are all common for students studying at University.

Maintaining a strong immune system is your first defence against picking up illnesses that will restrict your ability to study to your full potential. If you are regularly getting a cold or the flu, you will miss classes and get behind and that puts more pressure on your body through stress. Staying on top of things by keeping well will make your job of studying a lot easier and more enjoyable.

Caring for your body is simple - you need to take regular weekly exercise, be conscious of your posture when studying, eat a balanced moderate diet and ensure you get enough sleep.

Fitness

Having a certain amount of fitness will help you endure the rigours of life at University. A fit body will cope with physical stress a lot better than one that is unfit and overweight. An active body can study more efficiently than one that is inactive. A fit body generally has more energy than an unfit body so the physical strains have less effect. An unfit, unstimulated body will find it harder to muster the energy to get up early or to study late at night if it is required. So stay fit and active! You will find it a lot easier to study if you do. Eat plenty of fruit and vegetables and try to avoid too much fast food.

One of the biggest challenges I put my body through was when I left a Maths assignment until the very last week it was due. I remember saying to my friend 'It should only take us a few hours'. We didn't even leave it until the night before and we thought we had plenty of time. My friend and I spent 56 hours straight in the computer room at University working on the program. We hadn't realised how involved it was or how long it was going to take.

One of our very best friends came in a couple of times and brought us food. That was the only contact we had with the outside world. We were so tired by the end that we handed the assignment in (on time mind you) and then collapsed. I had to drive home that night which wasn't the smartest thing I ever did. We both looked terrible and felt even worse for the best part of a week and we both vowed we would never leave an assignment that late again.

To make things worse, when our assignments were returned, we had been marked down for having similar answers. Our lecturer had realised that we had worked on the assignment together, even though we had the right answers.

It's funny that in the work force, we are expected to work in a team and generate the very best possible outcome, while at University you can be penalised for working together and getting everything right!

Back Care

It is common while studying at University to complain of back, shoulder and neck pain. This can be due to a range of reasons but the most common are:

- Carrying a large bag full of books on your shoulder

- Sitting down at a desk for many hours at a time without breaks

- Not enough exercise to strengthen the muscles around the spine

- Bad posture whilst sitting down to study

If you can avoid any or all of these common habits then you may save yourself a lot of discomfort and many visits to a chiropractor / physiotherapist / osteopath. However, if you do suffer from pain or discomfort in your back, neck or shoulder region, it is important to get it seen to by a professional. Leaving it alone will not solve the problem and your practitioner will most likely highlight to you what habit you have that is causing it. They should also give you exercises to do to avoid having a recurrence.

Eye Care

Your eyes are another part of the body that tends to suffer while studying as they are used intensely to read volumes of written material. If you have to read a book or work on a computer for a long time, having regular breaks and allowing your eyes to focus on objects far away will lessen the strain. Making sure you have enough light will also help. It is prudent to have regular eye check-ups to ensure they remain healthy. If a problem does arise, it is better to be found and dealt with early.

I had a scare with my eyes after an exam, as I had been writing with my head about two inches above the desk for three hours. My eyes were fine during the exam but when I got up afterwards, I couldn't focus on anything more than 10 feet away! It lasted for about 10 minutes and I really thought I had done some damage. I went to the optometrist the next day and luckily everything was fine but I have never put my eyes under so much stress again.

Proper posture while using a computer helps to support your back and neck. Changing the focus of your eyes by looking at objects further away every once in a while will help adjust them and reduce the chances of eye strain.

Diet

Eating the right types of foods can help you feel great and along with exercise can reduce the amount of time you are sick. Try to eat a balanced diet that has a high nutritional content.

Relaxation

A regular massage on your back, neck and shoulders can do wonders for your mind as well as your body. I'm sure you will be able to find a friend who is willing to give you a massage in return for one and this could become a regular relaxation break for both of you. Don't be afraid to treat your body when it is feeling tired or after a big event like an exam period. The last thing your body will want is to go out and party all night. Save that for when you have a fully charged battery and will be able to enjoy it.

Sleep

It is important that you have enough sleep at night to recharge your body. Without it, you cannot function properly and you may feel irritable and unmotivated. Eight hours is an ideal amount of time to sleep each night, however some people need more sleep than others.

In the space below, write down how you will care for your body while you are studying at University.

I will care for my body at University by

_____

_____

_____

_____

_____

_____

There is a wealth of information on body care, fitness and nutrition on the Victorian Government's 'Go For Your Life' website at: **www.goforyourlife.vic.gov.au**

Summary

- *Caring for your body is an essential part of achieving and enjoying success*
- *Body care involves regular exercise, proper posture, a healthy diet and sleep*
- *Caring for your body can help keep you motivated*

Smoking, Drugs and Alcohol

Students who try drugs for the first time usually don't go out looking for them. More commonly, a friend, or someone they meet at a party offers them a sample. The decision to accept or reject the offer should not be made at the party or on campus while other students are around, as the full strength of peer group pressure will be hard at work.

A student who voices their own commitments regarding what they want or don't want to introduce into their own body should feel no guilt. There should be no emotion when answering the question firmly and no worry about what the reaction might be from the people around them. A firm answer is a strong answer and is less likely to be challenged.

The side effects of smoking and drugs are so negative and permanent that any student at University should take great care in making their decision. The addictive nature of both smoking and drugs, which are also widely publicised, should be an acute warning signal not to even try the most 'tame' versions of these abusive substances.

Binge drinking is also a trap for students at parties, although it is less common in later years. This type of substance abuse causes painful and damaging effects to body organs later in life. Short-term effects include hangovers and feeling sluggish for days after. These effects make it harder for students who want to do well.

Be choosy about the people you spend your time with and never be afraid to say what you feel.

> In the 5 years I spent at University between 1990 and 1995, I didn't see a single person taking drugs and nor was I ever offered drugs. I didn't feel the slightest bit left out by not associating with those who did.

First year students tend to be more vulnerable to such influences as they want to 'fit in' and be popular in their new environment. This is the perfect opportunity however, for you to take a strong stand and let your decision be known, if in fact you do get an offer to try something. Weaker personalities will always do what the crowd does. To be a successful student at University and stand out from your peers, you are going to need more than average ideals. You will need strong personal commitments and a determined character that allows you to say 'no' when you are offered something you don't want.

These activities are not recommended for students trying to get the most out of their University course and become a successful professional. There is nothing more unprofessional than seeing someone under the effects of drug or alcohol abuse.

Summary

- Be choosy about the people you spend your time with

- It's OK to say 'No'

- Never give in to peer group pressure – Have confidence to say what you mean

University Clubs and Facilities

University Clubs are a wonderful way to meet friends and experience a hobby or a sport while studying. Most students join a variety of clubs during their first year at University and then pursue those that suit their needs in the following years. As a past student of a University, you may be able to continue your membership of clubs and have full use of the equipment or facilities offered to current students.

The types of clubs available to students cover many interests from sports and languages through to arts and politics. The range is very broad and the fees for joining these clubs are usually minimal. There may also be reciprocal rights between clubs at different Universities. If a student is a member of a club at University, it may be possible for them to use the facilities or to join a team whilst visiting another University with reciprocal rights, without having to pay full joining fees.

Most Universities subsidise their clubs' funding, depending on the members they have by a certain time of the year. Generally, the clubs target first year students early on in the academic year when everything is new and exciting for them.

Be careful as a first year student that you are not persuaded to join too many clubs all at once at the start of your course. You are unlikely to have the time to pursue more than a handful of club activities. If you join too many clubs, you may overcommit yourself and risk losing interest altogether.

Find out a lot about the clubs you are interested in before you join any of them. Make sure their activities and functions will suit your timetable allowing you to make good use of all they have to offer. Ask students who have been members for a while about the types of activities they do. Make choices depending on which clubs you would really use, rather than what your friends are joining or what you would like to be *seen* joining.

Clubs at University are available to give you the opportunity to pursue a hobby or a sport. Spending time away from studies to follow an interest is beneficial to you as a student because it allows your mind and body to re-focus and gives you a more balanced lifestyle while studying. Most University clubs are started and run by students, so if the club you want to join is not available, you could make a proposal to the University to start the club yourself!

Most Universities have great facilities available to students and it may be beneficial for you to familiarise yourself with them so you can make time to use them. Sadly, many students go through their entire course unaware of the vast amounts of equipment and facilities they are able to use. Taking the time to discover what is available to you early on is a great advantage for your mind, your body and perhaps even your academic potential.

The facilities available to you at University are there for your enjoyment, relaxation and development. Enjoyment is beneficial for students because without it, life can become a chore and no one can perform at their peak in that environment. Physical and mental exercise outside the classroom is paramount to peak academic performance, as the oxygen intake that goes with it stimulates not only the body's muscles but also the brain. Relaxation is beneficial for students because it allows the body and mind to re-focus and avoid 'burnout'.

A student who studies all the time without having fun, taking exercise or relaxing, is more likely to suffer from fatigue and 'burnout' than those who spend time on other things and have a more balanced life at University. They will also tend to suffer from bad posture, which leads to discomfort and neural dysfunction. Mental fatigue is a common problem for students who don't take adequate breaks and try to keep studying when they are tired.

I must have spent at least 10 hours a week using the sporting facilities at University. I enjoyed the time away from reading and studying in the library. My classmates who didn't get away from their books often asked 'How can you spend so much time playing sport and still get good grades?' I told them I preferred to do something totally different and clear my mind before I sat down to study and I could never go straight from a class to the library because my mental ability to absorb information had disappeared after the lecture had finished! I always had to make time to recharge my mind before I studied.

There are many more facilities available to University students than most realise by the time they leave. There are obvious facilities like shops available on campus. When I first arrived, I couldn't believe that there was a grocery store, a cinema, a newsagency, a travel agent, a bank and a bookstore all in the heart of the campus. Many students don't have cars so it makes sense that all this is available.

When I joined the rock-climbing club and started to go out with the club on climbs all over the State, I assumed that someone in the club owned all the equipment we were using. It wasn't until months later that I realised the University had a shed full of equipment the club had bought over the years through funds from the club's annual membership fees.

There are many less obvious facilities like sporting and activity group equipment, career information and music listening libraries. They are there for you. Take the time to ask about them and look for facilities you can use while you are studying. Use them with moderation and never feel guilty for taking time out for enjoyment, exercise or relaxation. Each of these activities is beneficial and will be time well spent, adding balance to your life as a student at University.

Summary

- *University clubs and facilities are there for your use*
- *Join clubs that you have time for and will enjoy becoming involved in*
- *Some Universities have reciprocal rights with others around the world*

Image Protection

Your image is a part of you that will stay in people's minds for many years. It's amazing how people can recall what you did and what you were wearing when they met you. It's often said that 'a first impression is hard to change' and this is especially true when you go for a job interview. It is important to know the sort of person you want to be early on, so you can become that person as soon as possible. No one can truly morph from being a lazy irresponsible person one day to being a respectable, responsible, successful professional the next.

Similarly, 'a leopard never changes its spots'. In other words, if someone has a trait like laziness, unfaithfulness or dishonesty, it is very difficult for that person to ever be any different. It takes a lot of mental courage to face your own faults and not many people succeed in changing themselves. Of course some people do change but their past never does. The people who knew them with the bad trait often find it hard to forget and will usually associate that person in a bad light for many years.

It is important to protect your image as a University student, because the people you meet there may continue to be part of your career well after you graduate. In most industries, key players know each other and meet up at work places, seminars, job interviews and company start ups.

> A colleague at University was often asking me to show him my finished assignments so he could copy them without having to do any work himself. Of course I never gave them to him. I didn't see him after we graduated for a few years, until he came to my workplace for a job interview. My manager soon realised that we knew each other and asked me for a character assessment of him. I could only be honest about the experience I had with him at University. Needless to say, he didn't get the job.

Your lecturers at University are often there to give you a reference when you apply for your first jobs. If you make life hard for these people while you are a student at University, they are less likely to make an effort for you when you need them. If however you make life pleasant for your lecturers by simply being polite and courteous, they will more than likely go out of their way to help you. 'What comes around goes around' is a common sense saying that is useful to keep in the back of your mind.

Think about the sort of person you want to be and try to be that person every day of your life. You will never fully know who is watching you or with whom you will cross paths again later on. Therefore, keep it simple. Try to be polite, stay honest and look forward to your future knowing there are no spots on your back to hide when you graduate.

Summary

- A first impression is hard to change

- Be the person you want to be every day – 'What comes around, goes around'

- Be polite and stay honest – you never know who you'll bump into later on

What to Wear

Fashion is an enjoyable hobby for some but doesn't need to have too high a priority at University. Launching your life and career through your experience at University doesn't require you to be a fashion guru, unless you are studying fashion!

Make sure as a first priority that what you wear is comfortable. Secondly, your clothes should be chosen so that you will not be too hot or too cold during the entire day. If you need to take a sweater just in case you get cold, then take it. Alternatively, keep one in a locker at all times so you don't get caught out.

One of the worst consequences of not wearing the right type of clothes to University is that you get sick from having a compromised immune system. This leads to time off resulting in missed lectures, putting you behind in your course notes and your exam preparation. It is very difficult to catch up when you take time off due to illness.

Shoes are a very important item of clothing. You will walk many miles a week during your time at University as you will be moving between lectures and going to and from the stores to purchase meals and meet friends. Make sure your shoes are comfortable and will endure the high usage you will put them through.

I found it funny that in different parts of my University, students tended to wear different styles of clothes. You could almost tell which faculty a student was from by what they were wearing!

Fashion is a method that some students use to attract a partner. If you want to attract someone's attention at University, try not to use fashion as your main technique or you might attract him or her for the wrong reasons. Just try to be yourself. If that person wants to find out about you and spend time with you, the relationship will be well founded. You will then be able to knock him or her out when you do dress up on a date!

Summary

- *Wear clothes that are comfortable*
- *Make sure your shoes are sturdy and will endure high usage*
- *Keep a sweater on campus in case you need it*

Financial Budget

15

Finances

You will no doubt have higher expenses at University than you had at High School and it may be up to you to find the money to pay for them. These expenses may include rent, textbooks, petrol (gasoline), transport, board, food and levies charged by the University. You may also have a part-time job, scholarship, government assistance or allowance that offsets these expenses. For this reason, most University students learn to live on a budget for the first time in their lives as they start living by their own means. When you are just starting out as a student at University, you can't expect to have the best of everything and settling for second best for a while is the sensible thing to do.

The crucial thing to remember during your years at University is that the tight budgeting requirements are temporary and necessary. Getting yourself into high debt and living beyond your means can make life at University very difficult and can jeopardise your main aim or even the completion of your degree.

It is important to accept the financial limitations imposed on you while you are a student. You can't be working full-time and earning a full-time wage while you are studying. Therefore, you can't expect to live the life of a full-time employee and be able to buy all the things they can buy. This is a really basic idea but many students get trapped into debt and later regret using their credit card for things they didn't really *need*. Cars, stereo systems, DVDs, designer clothes, travel and mobile phones seem to be high-risk items students go into debt for.

Money difficulties can really change you. When you get into debt and discover the repayments force you to find another job or miss out on essentials, you become trapped in a vicious circle. Finding money for your short-term debt becomes more important than your main aim. The need to make regular repayments can damage your ability to study. Avoiding high debt while a student is far more sensible.

Planning

The graph on the following page, produced by the Commonwealth Bank of Australia, shows the typical income and expenses for people as they move through their lives. Take some time to understand the sections of this chart. It shows that at the age of 18, most students' income and expenses are very low compared with later on in their lives. It also shows that their income equals their expenses, which means the money young people earn is usually all spent. As they get older and by the time they reach the age of 30, the average person's expenses have increased considerably. Their income has also increased more than their expenses, so there is then enough money to cover expenses *and* have something left over to save for a bigger item like a deposit on a house.

While it is nice to have the best of everything throughout life, being a student at University is one time when you may have to curb your spending in order to stay afloat. For every item you consider buying, think about whether you can either live without it or buy it second hand. This avoids putting a financial noose around your neck while your income is limited.

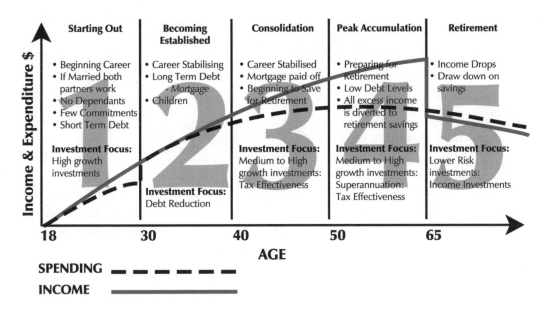

Figure 2: Typical Income and Expenditure over Lifetime.
(Graph courtesy of The Commonwealth Bank of Australia 2004)

Think about your income now and what you spend your money on. Are you paying any interest on your credit card? Are you having trouble making payments for something you don't really need? If this is your situation and your surplus income on the following page is negative, you will need to become organised and stop spending more money than you earn, as soon as possible.

Think about what items you spend your money on that you could do without. Your costs can simplistically be split into four categories Utilities, Entertainment, Habits and Impulses.

Utilities are the items you have to spend money on to get by including rent, petrol, transport, insurance, board and food.

Entertainment items are those you don't need but you choose to spend money on to make your life more enjoyable such as music, new clothes, club memberships, sports and socialising.

Habits are those items that you don't need but due to their ingredients and a lack of willpower, you buy because you are in the habit of doing so such as cigarettes, chocolate and alcohol.

Impulses are items you don't need and you don't go out to buy, but because you are at the shops; you see them, you like them and you buy them, often wondering why when you get back home. These include fashion items, nick knacks, snack food and jewellery.

You can only *save* money when you reduce your *Utilities* spending. By reducing your rent or power bill, you have *saved* money because an amount of money that was going to be spent anyway has been reduced.

You can't spend money in any other category and actually *save* money. Yet, how often do you hear people saying, 'I bought this shirt because it was on special so I saved $40!'?

On the following page, write down your weekly income from *any* source and compare it to your weekly expenses. How much do you have left over each week? How much *could* you have left over or how many hours could you not work if you reduced the amount of non-essential items you bought? All amounts in the table are weekly. This budget is available for downloading at

www.universitywisdom.com/budget

INCOME	Weekly Amounts	Totals
Income from source 1	1	
Income from source 2	2	
Income from source 3	3	
Income from all sources	**(Add 1+2+3)** ✎	**A**
ESSENTIAL EXPENSES		
Rent	4	
Textbooks	5	
University Fees	6	
Travel	7	
Petrol	8	
Board	9	
Basic Clothes	10	
Essential Telephone Bills	11	
Other Essential Expenses	12	
Total Essential Expenses	**(Add 4+5+6+7+8+9+10+11+12)** ✎	**B**
NON-ESSENTIAL EXPENSES		
Designer Clothes	13	
CDs / DVDs / Music	14	
Entertainment / Night Clubs	15	
Car Repayments	16	
Non Essential Telephone Bills	17	
Other Non Essential Expenses	18	
Total Non-Essential Expenses	**(Add 13+14+15+16+17+18)** ✎	**C**
SURPLUS INCOME	✎ **Now (A-B-C)**	✎ **Possible (A-B)**

Summary

● *Understand what you spend your money on*

● *Decide whether or not your are living within your means*

● *Complete a financial budget, stick to it and review it regularly*

Choosing Subjects

16

Students go to University for a great variety of reasons but generally, they want to have an enjoyable, fulfilling career after they graduate, which earns them a good income and the opportunity to do something worthwhile with their lives.

Most courses at University are made up of a set of core subjects and elective subjects. The core subjects are those you must pass in order to obtain your degree. You can then choose a number of elective subjects, which make up the balance of the points you need to graduate. Elective subjects are usually more specialised and are therefore often the most interesting to study.

Some core subjects are necessary stepping-stones to your career so don't be disappointed if there are some you are not entirely interested in. Getting through these subjects can be challenging but if you keep focused on the end result of obtaining your degree, you can find the energy and perhaps an inspiration to ensure you pass them.

It is important to have variety in the subjects you choose in order to keep your course interesting. If you choose a set of subjects that are all very similar, you may find that you get bored and lose interest. You may also be keeping your options open if you don't specialise in one area too early.

Students who choose subjects for higher financial rewards often don't enjoy their time at University as much, and enjoy their careers even less. This is because they have placed the value of money higher than the value of their education or lifestyle. These students often drop out of either their University course, or their careers early because they become stale and lack the desire to continue.

You need more than the incentive of money to do well in a career.

It's not *what* you learn that matters so much, it's *how you apply that knowledge*. Therefore, make sure you study what you're interested in and not what you think will make you more money.

> As a first year University student, I was expected to take subjects from all the different disciplines in engineering, including electrical, mechanical, computers, materials, chemical and civil. My decision to become a mechanical engineer came about because I enjoyed the mechanical subjects I took more than all the other subjects. I am still practising in mechanical engineering and really enjoy what I do.
>
> The advice I received as I was leaving school was 'It doesn't matter so much what you do, as long as you do it well'. This is still valid today and I would give that advice to anyone struggling to decide what course to take or what subjects to choose while at University. If you have enough passion for a topic, whether it is geography, engineering, biology, media studies, cleaning, warehousing, information technology or any other, you can take that career as far as you like.

So, if you find yourself choosing subjects because you think they will lead you to a higher salary or because one of your parents studied them, or someone told you they were 'easy', try to take a longer-term view of life and choose subjects because *you enjoy* them. They will more likely take you much further in the long run and give you the chance to enjoy your time at University as well as your career.

The way in which you choose subjects at University is critical to your enjoyment and prolonged interest as a student as well as after you graduate.

In the spaces below, rank how you will choose subjects at University.

My subject choices will be determined by:

	Strongly Disagree	Slightly Disagree	Not Fussed	Slightly Agree	Strongly Agree
My Passions	❏	❏	❏	❏	❏
My Teachers	❏	❏	❏	❏	❏
Subjects I will do well in	❏	❏	❏	❏	❏
Financial potential	❏	❏	❏	❏	❏
Subjects parents/friends took	❏	❏	❏	❏	❏

Summary

- *Find out which subjects are compulsory and which are elective*
- *You need more than the incentive of money to do well in a career*
- *Mix up a variety of subjects to make your course balanced and interesting*

Mutual Respect

17

The power of the mind and thoughts are not well understood. However it is very well known that your mind can work for you or against you, depending on whether you use it in a positive or a negative way. Using your mind in a positive way can have spectacular results.

'Don't look down' is a very well known phrase in the sport of climbing. It is used to keep someone's mind focused on what is available (i.e. the rock around them and the rope, which provides all the support and protection they need), rather than what is *not* underneath them. The natural tendency for new climbers is to look down as they move up the rock. This can be unnerving and cause their mind to take over their physical ability, by unbalancing their thought patterns. This mental destabilisation can cause a mental block as they work through the 'what if I fall' scenarios. Although they are physically capable of making the climb, their mind does not allow it.

The same phrase and ideas about the power of the mind can be related to the attitude of University students. However, unlike climbers who use it against the reaction of fear, it should be used against yet another powerful feature of the mind – the ego.

Egos play a very important role in shaping the attitude of people. Without a balanced ego, people can become mentally unstable. A person with a low ego can become very insecure or depressed and one whose ego is overcooked can be arrogant and tend to look down on the people around them.

"Doubt is not a pleasant condition, but certainty is absurd."
Voltaire (1694 - 1778)

One of the most detrimental lessons you can 'learn' at University is that you will come out with your degree and be a better person than those without one. Sadly, this is a reality for some students and they wonder why they lose their friends and find it hard to get a job after they graduate. Thinking you will be a better person or be more successful just because you have a University degree is far from the truth. Friends and employers will sense your inflated ego a mile away and you may lose a lot of business, potential friendships and work colleagues' respect, if that is how you plan to think. Having mutual respect for what other people choose to do with their lives is a far more balanced approach and will allow you to work effectively with a wider variety of people.

Being able to work with all kinds of people is a very marketable skill, especially from an employer's point of view. No matter how clever you are, if you can't work in a group environment and allow the company to benefit from your talents, they would be better off hiring someone less talented who has those skills.

"Politeness and consideration for others is like investing pennies and getting dollars back." Thomas Sowell (1930 -), Creators Syndicate

Many new managers in business lose the respect of their colleagues, as they believe they were promoted because they were better than everyone else. Being a manager is a job that suits some people and not others. Some employees are worth too much in another position to be lost to a management role. Being a manager takes a certain type of person, *not* a better type of person.

During my engineering work experience at the local sewage farm, I did general engineering office work until my final two weeks, when I asked to go down into the engine room and work alongside the crew who maintained the plant. I was thrilled when management agreed and excitedly went downstairs with my cap and overalls on.

On my first day in the engine room with the mechanics, I was asked a lot of questions about what I was doing at University and what I wanted to learn while I was with the maintenance crew. I was given plenty of opportunity to elevate myself – after all, none of them had a University degree. Instead, I turned the conversation around and asked about their experiences.

As I did not put myself up on a pedestal, I became one of the team. I was able to work with them, joke with them and very soon, they forgot that I was an engineering student. I was just like any other apprentice, which is what I wanted. I learnt more in those two weeks about engineering than I did in the other 3 months, because I was learning new skills and it was all 'hands on'. I had people around me who were willing to teach me and wanted me to learn about what they did. They had pride in their skills because I was genuinely interested in them.

I became aware of a huge barrier between the engineers/managers and the maintenance crew. The main problem the workers had with the management and engineers was their ATTITUDE and their belief that they were better people because of their positions and qualifications.

Of course it takes all types to make this world function and the sewage plant wouldn't be running if it weren't for those guys with the practical skills to keep it operating. I will be eternally grateful to them for their patience and their honesty. They confirmed my ideas about everyone needing respect for their part in life and as a consequence, I have always had a great working relationship with employees on all rungs of the ladder and from all walks of life.

Treating others the way you would like to be treated is a great starting point for success in interpersonal skills. You will not only gain more respect and find jobs more easily but you will also have a better working relationship with your colleagues and enjoy your course and career more.

Remember that your mind is more powerful than any other part of you. Make it work for you, the company you work for and the colleagues you work with. Resist the temptation to allow your ego to put a gap between you and your friends or family. Share your knowledge as the benefits of generosity will flow back to you in many ways and others will do the same for you.

Summary

- *Use your mind in a positive way - 'Don't look down' on others*
- *Keep a healthy respect for yourself and for others around you*
- *Share your knowledge to experience the benefits of your own generosity*

PART 3

How will you get there?

Time Management

Time management is probably one of the most important aspects of success. Without the ability to organise what you are going to do and when, your experience at University may seem like a never ending race to get things done. The pressure on your time may sometimes be immense, especially if you are undertaking a course with a high contact commitment. Time management is just as important when you are out in the work force or running a business, so it is a very valuable skill to develop while you are at University.

There are many ways of managing your time when you are under pressure to perform. Having your commitments under control makes life at University a whole lot easier. There is little chance that you will ever be able to keep track of everything you need to do in your head. There will be many assignments with due dates, meetings, tutes and excursions to keep track of. Without a method to keep all of this under control, you will most likely miss important information, especially if you miss lectures or tutes. You may lose marks for not handing in assignments by their due date and apart from making life unnecessarily hard for yourself, you can lower your possible level of success by being disorganised.

There are many tools available for time management, including diaries, calendars and computer programs such as Microsoft Outlook®. There are also time lines and other formal systems: find a system that works for you. Not everyone uses all the tools for time management, but everyone who manages their time gets more things done, with less effort, than those who don't.

The challenge for students at University who have many assignments is not generally the complexity of the assignments themselves: students usually find that the race against time is the hardest part of completing assignments. Students tend to hold off starting an assignment until they feel they have to. Not many students will begin an assignment the day they receive it, even though most will know they should.

A couple of times I handed in assignments in a rush and realised within an hour or two that I had made a silly mistake. It was so frustrating and I kicked myself for literally throwing away marks. That was a sign of bad time management because I would have picked up the mistake before I'd handed it in if I'd finished the work earlier and given myself time to read it through.

Set aside regular time slots to work on assignments, from the day you receive them until they are due. Get a good proportion of them done early on and you should avoid the predicament of having a mad rush before any due dates.

Summary

- *There are many tools available to help you manage your time*
- *Students need to use time management skills to win the race against time*
- *Always leave time to review assignments before you hand them in*

Using a Diary

19

Diaries can help you arrange your time so you don't find yourself needing to be in two places at once. They allow you to pre-plan, so your life doesn't become a last minute rush. Everything you have to do and want to do is right there in front of you.

Diaries also allow you to organise your time so that your goals can physically get done. Be practical when you assign time slots and always allow for travel time in between if you need to move from place to place.

You can add milestones into your diary to break more complex goals into smaller tasks and set down a time frame for doing each. Complex goals require more planning, as some milestones can't be achieved until others have been.

Diaries are also a great record of what you have done in the past. If you ever have to look up an event or a certain date, your life and past goals are all there - what you did, who you saw, where you went.

It doesn't matter whether you use an electronic diary or a paper diary, just as long as you use a diary. Writing things down as they happen and having the ability to plan your time is essential for you to be able to function and get things done in order and on time.

> I would have been totally lost without my diary while I was at university. I remember some people gasping when I opened it, as they couldn't believe how many items were in it. Admittedly, my life at university was busy. However, I wouldn't have done half the things I did without the help of my trusty diary.
>
> My diary went everywhere with me and helped me get my assignments in on time. It helped me plan my sporting and social time. I wrote in my work shifts at the pool so I would be prepared and could plan study time around them. I also put in when I was tutoring after class. At one stage I was tutoring 15 students who were all doing High School Maths. That definitely took some organising!

If you don't have a diary, you will need to start using one. I don't know how anyone can function without one. An easy answer when an opportunity arises is 'No, I don't have time'. If you actually look in your diary and see when you do have some time, you'll be surprised how much you can fit into your life.

It is very disheartening to see someone arrive to a class where everyone else is handing in an assignment and they have forgotten all about it. Guard yourself against that ever happening to you by writing everything in your diary - *as it happens*. Don't try to use your memory to write things in when you get home. If you enter them straight away and refer to your diary regularly, you should avoid waking up in the middle of the night wondering if you have done everything you needed to do that day.

Using a diary is easy and you'll probably wonder how you ever coped without one.

Diary entries don't have to be all about work or study. An important goal at University is to use your diary to find time to do things you enjoy. Find some time in your diary when you can squeeze in an hour or two, just for you. You will have many demands on your time where lecturers will want this assignment or that 'prac' written up and submitted by a certain date. By pre-planning your weeks to allow for example a game of squash with a friend each Thursday night, you will have something to look forward to during the week.

Take a look at a couple of pages from my diary while I was a student at University.

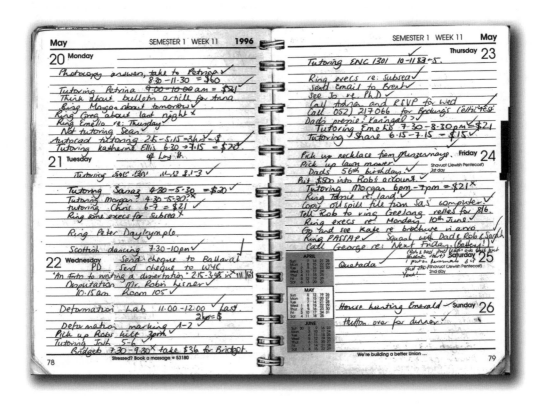

Notice how items are not crossed out when they are completed. They are simply ticked or crossed on the side depending on whether or not they were completed. It is often useful to be able to go back through old diaries for one reason or another to see what you did and when you did it. I still have my diaries right back to when I was in High School. They are both interesting and amusing.

Notice also that when a week has past, the bottom right hand corner of the diary page is cut off. That is a very useful trick, as the diary will then automatically open on the current weeks page when you open it.

I know I wouldn't be able to do half of what I do without my diary. Once something is written down, it becomes a commitment. It is a reminder you see every day. When you use your diary efficiently, you might begin to enjoy ticking off items – every time I do, I have an incredible sense of achievement and satisfaction.

Your ability to get things done by using a diary will be astonishing.

Pretty well all the pages of my diaries for the last fifteen years have looked like this one. Now you can understand why some people get so much done. They are not especially talented, they just have a winning formula and they use it every day.

Here is another page from the same diary, later on in the year. Notice how the style of entries is still the same.

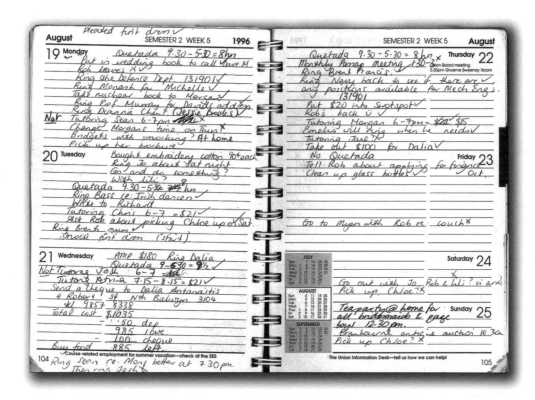

Once a date has past, you are not likely to look at that page in your diary again. You are more likely to look at pages in the future to see what has to be done. That is why assignments must be written in your diary at least twice. The 80% and 2-Day Rule® explained in Chapter 20 will give you a simple way to organise your assignments in your diary.

Once using a diary becomes a habit, it only makes life easier as it is like having a personal assistant, constantly reminding you of what you need to do and when. More importantly, diaries allow you to organise the things you want to do. I would choose order over chaos any day – wouldn't you?

Summary

- *A diary allows you to plan your assignments, commitments and entertainment*
- *Use a tick next to any accomplished tasks in your diary*
- *Keep your diary with you - then you can write things down as they happen*

8̶0̶% and 2-Day Rule®

The 80% and 2-Day Rule® will save you a lot of heartache when you have assignments due to be handed in on a certain date. The 80% and 2-Day Rule® is simple – anyone can do it. The idea is that when you are given an assignment, you immediately determine the dates it should be finished, reviewed and printed, and enter those dates into your diary.

Write down the date the assignment is due. Then write down the number of days you have left to work on it, on every date, between the day after you receive the assignment and the day you should finish working on it. The latter date is when 80% of the total available time is used up.

Therefore, if you are given 10 weeks to complete the assignment, you allow 8 weeks for actually doing the work. The last two weeks are assigned to completing the final copy. This must be completed and printed out by the 'drop-dead date', which is 2 days before the assignment is due.

You might be wondering why you want to complete an assignment a clear 2 days before it is due. Well, there are at least two good reasons.

The first is, there is nothing more frustrating than to complete an assignment 30 seconds before it is due and as you walk away after handing it in, you realise you have made a mistake. There is no explanation for this but poor time management and if you can get your assignments finished early, you will have plenty of time to re-read them and find any silly mistake you have made, well before you hand it in.

Another good reason is that printing out an important assignment usually involves a hiccup or two. No matter whose printer you use, it may jam, run out of ink or paper and you will need to fix this before you have a copy of your assignment in your hand. If you use a printer at the University, *everyone else* will want to print their assignments too.

You only have to be in a printing room half an hour before a major assignment is due to realise the benefit of the 80% and 2-Day Rule®. Due dates are a very stressful time and thankfully, I was only caught once in this situation. Forever after, I made sure I had my assignments finished at least two days ahead of schedule.

Here is a simple exercise for you to understand the 80% and 2-Day Rule®.

Imagine you are given an assignment on the 4th October, that has to be handed in on the 14th November.

How many days have you got to do the assignment?   _____ days.

(Hint, don't include the first or last days but do include all weekends)

Now calculate what 80% of that time is   _____ days.

What date do you aim to have the assignment finished?   _____

What is the 'drop-dead date', or the date it must be printed?   _____

Answers

27 days in October

13 days in November

40 days in Total

80% of 40 = 32 days

■ *Receive Assignment = 4ᵗʰ October*

■ *Time to work on Assignment (31 days) = 5ᵗʰ October – 4ᵗʰ November*

■ *Aim to finish on 4ᵗʰ October + 32 days = 5ᵗʰ November*

■ *Time to review Assignment (6 days) = 6ᵗʰ November – 11ᵗʰ November*

□ *Drop dead date = 14ᵗʰ November – 2 = 12ᵗʰ November*

○ *Due date = 14ᵗʰ November*

October 2005						
M	T	W	Th	F	Sa	Su
					1	2
3	4	5 32	6 31	7 30	8 29	9 28
10 27	11 26	12 25	13 24	14 23	15 22	16 21
17 20	18 19	19 18	20 17	21 16	22 15	23 14
24 13	25 12	26 10	27 9	28 8	29 7	30 6
31 6						

November 2005						
M	T	W	Th	F	Sa	Su
	1 5	2 4	3 3	4 2	5 1	6
7	8	9	10	11	12 Print	13
14 DUE	15	16	17	18	19	20
21	22	23	24	25	26	27
28	29	30				

Download your own University Wisdom Calendar at
www.universitywisdom.com/calendar

Summary

- *The 80% and 2-Day Rule® allows you to plan assignments using your diary*
- *Use 80% of the given time to do your assignment*
- *Review your assignment and print it out at least 2 days before it is due*

oal Setting

A powerful tool to help ensure your goals are achieved is a 'to do' list. This is simply a list of goals you want to complete. There is no need for the list to be in a specific order but you should put a priority against all items to rank their importance.

Your 'to do' list can be added to and changed at any time. Once a task is achieved, it is important not to erase it. Simply tick the task off or put a line through it. By erasing it totally, you may feel like you are starting from scratch with your list and you will soon forget about all the tasks you have achieved. Leaving the items you have ticked shows you that you are making progress and gives you a powerful sense of achievement.

A 'don't do' list is just as useful. Think of all the things you do regularly that you wish you didn't. Do you ever kick yourself after aimlessly watching hours of television? I certainly do. If you know what you're doing that you shouldn't be doing and you write one or two of them down, you may find that you actively stop doing them. This is because by writing them down, you make a subconscious decision to stop doing them.

Using goal setting as a regular tool is a simple but powerful way to make life at University less stressful, as your goals will be easier to achieve.

Write down some goals you'd like to achieve, stating a priority of 1 to 5 for each:

Priority of 1= Important, 5 = Trivial

Three goals you'd like to achieve this week: Priority

    1. _____ _____

    2. _____ _____

    3. _____ _____

Three goals you'd like to achieve this month:

    4. _____ _____

    5. _____ _____

    6. _____ _____

Three goals you'd like to achieve this year:

    7. _____ _____

    8. _____ _____

    9. _____ _____

Three goals you'd like to achieve by the time you finish University:

    10. _____ _____

    11. _____ _____

    12. _____ _____

Now you have 12 goals to set out and do in order of priority. It is so easy! If you can achieve only half of what you have written down, you are well on the way to using this tool to become more successful.

Write down one complex goal that seems unattainable:

13. _____

Now break this complex goal down into *at least three* achievable goals:

14. _____
15. _____
16. _____
17. _____
18. _____
19. _____

Write down three things you do as a habit that you wish you didn't:

20. _____
21. _____
22. _____

You now have a 'to do' list and a 'don't do' list.

Consider how will you go about achieving all these goals now they are written down.

Summary

- *Use a 'to do' list to organise and prioritise your goals*
- *Use a 'don't list' to commit to giving up habits you shouldn't have*
- *Break down complex goals into a series of achievable ones*

Focus

22

Focus is a skill which enables you to concentrate entirely on a single task for as long as it takes to complete. Having the ability to focus is essential while studying at University. It is far more effective to work on one task at a time, enabling you to concentrate more thoroughly and produce a better result on each. Your ability to retain the information you learn should also be much higher if you separate your work and focus on each task individually.

It would take a genius to effectively work on two assignments from different subjects at the same time.

A useful tip for ensuring you focus your attention is to clear your desk of all other material while you are working on one subject. If you have a mixture of other textbooks and notes, mail and newsletters in view while you are trying to work, your eyes may catch this other material and your focus can temporarily be lost.

Only having the relevant material in view will enable your mind to focus fully on the one subject. You will most likely finish what you are doing more quickly and to a higher standard.

Try this simple exercise:

1. Sit down and use your right hand to draw a number six in the air in front of you. Repeat drawing this six, 10 times.

2. Now lift your right foot off the ground and make a circle in a clockwise direction. Repeat making this circle, 10 times.

3. Think about how easy both those tasks were. Now...

4. Rotate your right leg in a clockwise direction again as in step 2.

5. At the same time, draw the number six in the air with your right hand.

What happened to your leg?

What happened to the shape of the circle?

What happened to the quality of the six you drew?

Without lots of practice, it is almost impossible to do two different tasks well, no matter how simple, if you try to do them at the same time. This is especially true at University, as the tasks are generally complex and full concentration is required to complete them. Learning to focus on one task at a time using a clutter-free work space, can help you achieve this.

Summary

• *Separate your assignments into discrete, manageable tasks*

• *Use a clear workspace for each task so you can focus on them one at a time*

• *Free up your time by working efficiently and effectively*

Time Line

A time line is a simple method of *vaguely* sketching your life plan so that you have a window into the future. It is not a list set in concrete, but can be updated at any stage in your life. A time line is a useful tool for people who have lots of goals they want to achieve. It allows for these goals to be set out in a logical timely order.

A time line is a projection, where you arrange your life in yearly increments. Each goal is given its required time so that everything can be planned for. It also sets in writing when your lifestyle changes are due such as being a student, working and retirement. This allows you to plan for financial requirements so these events don't just creep up and surprise you when you are in your sixties. People who don't plan for their retirement often get a shock when they reach retirement age. They wonder where their life went and often fall into retirement without any goals achieved or enough money to live the way they'd like to.

Having a plan is not boring - it is a powerful tool to help you achieve your goals. Without knowing *what* you want to do, how will you know that you are achieving your goals? How will you ever fit everything you want to do in your life if you don't plan ahead? Time lines are very exciting because your goals are laid out in black and white and you can work towards making them happen.

The time line below depicts my high priority goals until I reach the age of 60. I am sure I will add to them in the future as my life evolves.

Year	Age	Goal(s)
2005	34	Create and market University Wisdom
2006	35	Print University Wisdom and send a copy to every High School in Australia
2007	36	Help other people achieve financial freedom. Stop full-time work
2008	37	Be involved in my children's school and education
2009	38	Be involved in my children's school and education
2010	39	Be involved in my children's school and education
2011	40	Be involved in my children's school and education
2012	41	Be involved in my children's school and education
2013	42	Be involved in my children's school and education
2014	43	Be involved in my children's school and education
2015	44	Be involved in my children's school and education
2016	45	Be involved in my children's school and education
2017	46	Be involved in my children's school and education
2018	47	Be involved in my children's school and education
2019	48	Be involved in my children's school and education
2020	49	Be involved in my children's school and education
2021	50	Travel the world with my husband and children for fun
2022	51	Travel the world with my husband and children for fun
2023	52	Try property development
2024	53	Try property development
2025	54	Visit Antarctica
2026	55	Tour around Australia with my husband
2027	56	Tour around Australia with my husband
2028	57	Help budding entrepreneurs get ideas off the ground

Year	Age	Goal(s)
2029	58	Help budding entrepreneurs get ideas off the ground
2030	59	Help budding entrepreneurs get ideas off the ground
2031	60	Help budding entrepreneurs get ideas off the ground

Of course I don't expect my life to end at age 60 – one of my life goals is to live to 100!

My personal time line helps me arrange my goals in a vague sequence. I can update this at any time if my goals change.

In the following table, try to create a time line for yourself for the next 25 years. You will have to give thought to how many years each goal will take to achieve and the order in which you want to achieve them.

Year	Age	Goal(s)
2006		
2007		
2008		
2009		
2010		
2011		
2012		
2013		
2014		
2015		
2016		
2017		
2018		
2019		
2020		
2021		
2022		
2023		
2024		
2025		
2026		
2027		
2028		
2029		
2030		

Summary

- A time line gives you a window into your future
- Your goals can be changed at any time depending on your circumstances
- Look forward to achieving the goals you set yourself!

Form Good Habits

Think of habits as either good or bad. If they are good habits, they will make you slowly but surely better health-wise, financially, or happier. If they are bad habits, again, they will make you slowly but surely less healthy, financially worse-off or less happy. When habits are formed, it is only a matter of time before the consequences of the habits start to appear.

By forming habits, you can adjust your lifestyle to do almost anything. The idea is to eliminate your bad habits and ingrain in your lifestyle a whole series of good habits that will take you far beyond your wildest dreams. While average habits keep most people average, good habits take others one-step at a time towards success and a very enjoyable lifestyle.

If you read about how many of the world's most successful people achieved their goals, you will find most of them describe the habits they formed that eventually led them to where they are. For most, it was a slow process but an easy one because they found a winning formula and stuck to it.

Think about all the habits you have and try to work out which ones are good and which ones are bad. In the space below, write them down in point form. To define a habit, it must be something that you do regularly, either daily or at least once a week. Some examples of habits are:

Going for a walk, phoning friends, smoking, watching television, saving money, going to the pub.....
Remember, some habits may seem unproductive but they may still be good habits as they allow you to relax and re-focus. An example of this type of habit may be reading comics.

MY GOOD HABITS	MY BAD HABITS

What are the habits you'd like to stop and the habits you'd like to start? Most people have habits they know are bad and shouldn't do. Only by writing them down can you identify them and then work towards eliminating or reducing them.

Write down in the following spaces what habits you would like to eliminate and those you would like to start. By writing them down, you will have already made the first step towards achieving your goal.

GOOD HABITS I WANT TO START	BAD HABITS I WANT TO STOP
Start using a diary	Stressing about things that I can't change!
Find a place for my...	

In order to write this book, I knew I had to form a habit and just do a little bit at a time. I didn't have the opportunity to sit in my office without interruptions and write from the start to the end. So doing a little bit often is exactly what I've done. When you set out to write a book, it is a daunting task. Breaking it down into parts and then chapters makes the whole idea a lot more manageable. Committing to the habit of writing a small amount each day was the only way this book has been possible. This commitment to doing something small regularly is how most large achievements are made.

Habits help you achieve your goals in small regular steps

Habits can be used to slowly work your way towards any goal. Your goal may be to save up for a car. If you put away only a small amount of money regularly, your car will soon eventuate, as long as you stick to the habit of making regular contributions. The easiest way of doing this is to make the payments automatically and then make extra payments when you can. (Speak to your bank if you are not sure how to do this).

Habits can also save you many hours of unproductive time. Think of how many hours you spend each week looking for items such as car keys, wallets, handbags or mobile phones. Think about how annoyed you get when you lose these items, especially when you are in a hurry or are holding someone else up while you look for them. A simple habit to avoid all this is to have a set place for each of these items. All you have to do is put the items in their place every time you put them down. Then, they will be there when you need them and you have eliminated the need to search for them. Bingo – problem solved, by using a simple habit.

One of my most useful habits has been to utilise the time I spend in my car driving to and from work. Like most people, I usually listen to the radio, but I have started to occasionally listen to CDs I can learn from. Many books that are published in a printed format are also published on an audio CD. You then listen to a person reading the book, so you can effectively 'read' while you are driving. One of the more useful CDs I have 'read' this way five times!

For this reason, *University Wisdom* is also available in audio format from:

www.universitywisdom.com

Summary

- *There are good habits and bad habits*
- *Only good habits can take you closer to wherever it is you want to go*
- *Eliminating bad habits can help you get there faster*

Communicate and Act Promptly

Acting promptly to deal with a problem that requires attention is the only way to stay on top of it and move on. This applies to being a student at University as well as a worker or a business owner. As the old saying goes 'Never let a problem fester'. Many people are controlled by their problems and do nothing about them, then wonder why the problem is worse later on. Others prefer to take control of problems, find solutions and get on with the job in the shortest amount of time.

When study becomes confusing, as it tends to do from time to time, it's important to keep your queries under control and not let them mount up or get lost over time. You would have to be super human to understand every concept from each and every subject, so it is highly likely that you will need some guidance along the way.

Learn to ask questions so you can deal with problems as soon as possible

There is no point blaming your lecturer for being a bad teacher. Lecturers come in many different flavours and all have different styles of teaching. Your lecturer will be your first point of call if you need clarification on subject matter. If you build up a negative mental picture of your lecturer, you will not do anything but cut off your ability to draw information out of him or her. Part of becoming a fully mature person is accepting the differences in the people you work with and having the ability to ask questions when you don't understand something.

Acting promptly when you get confused is your first defence against problems spiralling out of control. If you have written down a note that doesn't make sense during a lecture, approach your lecturer afterwards to see if you can get the explanation you require. It may only take a minute and will save you a lot of heartache later on. If you don't get what you require then and there, you may ask your lecturer to give you 10 minutes of his or her time when it is mutually convenient.

This type of approach can be far more productive than leaving the question until weeks later when the concept is far from your mind. Asking questions during lectures is also a great help when you don't understand what is said. Always listen to other student's questions and listen to the answers given by the lecturer as you can learn a lot from these discussions.

Think about the following problems you could encounter as a student at University and decide how long you should wait before you deal with them:

                                                                      (Circle the time frame)

1.   You don't understand something your lecturer says in class   _____ mins/hrs/days

2.   You miss a day and have to catch up on class notes   _____ mins/hrs/days

3.   You are having trouble with an assignment due in two weeks   _____ mins/hrs/days

Summary

- *Acknowledge confusion or the need for review when it happens*
- *Seek out the appropriate help*
- *Control your problems so they don't control you*

Learn from Others

Learning from others is a short cut way to accelerate your understanding while you are at University. Listening to other students' questions and the answers they receive is a great use of your time, even if you are not entirely familiar with what is being said. The topics of discussions held during class should be relevant to your course and therefore, what you learn by listening may be relevant to your homework, exams or an assignment.

> I noticed that the students who asked most of the questions in class were up to date with their homework and assignments. They often did really well in tests so they were people you could learn a lot from.
>
> When they asked questions about homework I hadn't even started, it was still very helpful to listen to the questions and answers. By the time I did that homework myself, and got to the questions that had been discussed in class, it made more sense.
>
> It was easy to work out who hadn't listened to these discussions in class as they asked the same questions later on. So don't just switch off when someone else asks a question - try to learn from both the question and the answer.

It is also important in lectures to *watch your lecturer talking*. You can get just as much information about the topic by watching your lecturer's eyes and facial expressions, as you can from just writing everything down as it goes up on the board.

A lot of students miss really important information because they don't watch as well as listen. When a lecturer tries to stress a point or focus on something that is obviously important, they usually raise their eyebrows, look at someone intently who is watching them, point to a particular item they have written on the board or pause silently.

If you miss making a note of these cues, then you may miss something that could possibly (and probably will) be on the exam. Not all lecturers are this animated, however the majority of them are.

> I used to put a star next to the point that was being highlighted in my notes even though I wasn't always sure what the relevance of the point was. If I knew the lecturer was highlighting a particular equation or idea, I made sure that when I opened my notebook the points were immediately obvious.
>
> When it came time to study for my exams, I thoroughly researched the highlighted equations and ideas as I read through my textbooks. More often than not, they were used as main examination topics. I was often really glad I'd spent a little effort in class noticing the cues made by the lecturer.

Learning from others is not only a simple method of accelerating your understanding; it can make a huge difference in your marks at the end of the year. This is quite distinct from copying other students' work. Copying other students' work will leave you with less understanding and you will be caught out later on when your understanding is tested during an exam or in the work force. Do yourself a favour and avoid copying at all costs. Stay alert in class and listen to other students' questions and the answers they receive. Watch your lecturer's expressions and signals. Above all, if you have a question of your own, don't hold back waiting for someone else to ask it, act promptly and ask it yourself.

Summary

- *Listen to other students' questions and the answers they are given*
- *Learn to read signals from your lecturer when they highlight important points*
- *Avoid copying at all costs – it will always catch up with you*

Using a Computer

The power of computers is hard to grasp, until you start using them effectively. Computers are not only useful for students studying courses requiring calculations. Learning the skills to use a computer competently is beneficial for anyone studying at University. Even farmers use computers these days!

Don't be fooled. A computer won't do the work for you. You still have to spend time on your tasks and think about what you are doing in order to successfully complete them. What your computer can do however is allow you to complete tasks more efficiently.

Once you master the basic skills of using a computer, you may be astounded at what other tasks computers can help you with. I have been using computers for over twenty years and am still finding new ways of using them to help me.

The power of a computer is hard to quantify without using a real example. Test yourself here by working out the result of an equation. If you don't understand the maths, just imagine you do understand it and try to guess how long it would take you to work the problem out.

The first time you try this, you are not allowed to use any form of computer, not even a calculator. The second time you do the calculation, you are allowed to use a calculator.

In this problem you have to find the value of X, knowing the values of a, b and c.

If $X=2(a+5)+3(4-b)-(8+c)$

where $a=3$, $b=1$ and $c=8$

Write your answers to the question in the spaces below. Don't forget to time yourself!

Answer for X using no computer or calculator

X = _____   Time taken = _____ minutes _____seconds

Answer for X using a calculator

X = _____   Time taken = _____ minutes _____seconds

When you look at your two sets of results, are your values of X the same? What is the difference in the times?

We can work with my own results to complete this example. My two answers were the same (and I should hope so, since I have a degree in Mathematics!) and X = 9.

The time it took me to complete the calculation without a computer or calculator was 20 seconds. The time it took me with a calculator was 18 seconds. Comparing those two results, I would be better off to use a calculator since it was faster for me and gave me the same answer.

A computer would do that calculation in **less than 1 second**.

When using a computer, it is important to save your files to a removable backup device regularly so that in the event of a computer 'crash', you will still have a fairly recent copy. Losing hours of work is bad enough, but losing an assignment that took you weeks to write is very inconvenient and should be avoided at all costs.

Here are some differences between having and not having access to a computer from a University students' perspective. As you can see, life can be much more efficient with a computer.

Having access to a computer while studying	Not having access to a computer while studying
My time will be used more efficiently with a computer.	I will take much longer to complete my tasks.
Forces me to learn to type, which is a useful tool in the work force as well as life in general.	Makes learning to type difficult.
Makes it easier and quicker for me to change assignments and present professional work.	Changes will be done by hand and this could take a very long time. Unless my hand writing skills are good, my work may become messy.
I can use my computer to access the Internet for research.	I will have to find books at the library for all my research.

Computer Access

There are many ways you can gain access to a computer. You can borrow a friend's computer, use the computers available at the University, buy a brand new computer, buy a second hand computer, lease a computer or use a computer available at the local library.

Like anything, there are advantages and disadvantages between the different ways of accessing a computer. Some cost money, while others don't. Some allow you to access the computer any time you like and some have restricted access.

Whichever way you decide to access a computer, keep in mind that the computer is there to make your life easier. Get to know it like a friend and it may help you more than you could ever imagine. It might be difficult at first but with persistence and patience with both yourself and the computer, you will learn to appreciate the benefits it offers.

A computer is not something to be afraid of. Millions of people use computers every day and the number of computer users worldwide just keeps growing and growing. It is never too late to start using a computer. Someone probably used one to find this book for you!

Summary

- A computer can make your work and research at University more efficient
- Save your work regularly to a removable backup device
- Good computer skills is an advantage at University as well as in the work force

Using the Internet

The Internet – What It Is

The Internet is a worldwide connection of millions of computers. Anyone with access to one of these computers can view and interact with the information on public display on any of the other connected computers. The Internet is an exciting, opportunity-rich environment.

The Internet is used by people to shop, do banking, write to friends, book holidays and find distant relatives to name a few. Students use it mainly as a researching tool. Businesses use the Internet to display and sell their products and services.

A Search Tool

The power of the Internet is enormous and can make a task like researching for an assignment at University very simple. The information is accessible from a computer, so you don't need to travel to a library and search through rows of books. The hardest part is usually deciding when to stop looking for information and start using what you find in your assignments.

There would be very few topics where a search engine would turn up nothing. People all around the world are continually writing information and displaying it on the Internet for the public to read. So the amount of information available on the Internet is continually growing.

If for example you want to find information about a particular company, group or University, the quickest and most direct way would be to look them up on the Internet. There, you will find all the information they want the public to have access to and if there is something more you need, there should also be a way of contacting them either by phone, email or an enquiry form.

The Internet is not a verifiable source of information

If you are searching for information you need to rely on, remember that *anything* can be published on the Internet by *anyone*. What you read on the Internet could have been written by an expert, *or by someone who knows nothing about the topic*. It is important to always try to search for legitimate sites where you can contact the writer if you need to ask questions or verify information you want to use. If no contact information is available, be very cautious about using the information provided.

A Warning

Unrelated advertising on a website is designed to distract your attention to another site in the hope you will buy a product or service on impulse. As part of the deal with the host site (the site where the advert sits), the advertiser may have access to any information you send through to the host site, if you fill in any forms.

Spam and spyware is unsolicited email and software that sits on your computer and can send out information about you and your computer to people you don't know. These programs can get onto your computer via the Internet or by email.

Never open an email or any attachment to an email if you don't recognise the sender. You should 'block' the email and web address and the email itself should be deleted along with any attachments. The 'deleted' email folder on your computer should then be emptied immediately. Don't ever let unsolicited emails or attachments sit in your deleted folder as they are still physically on your computer and are capable of being run accidentally.

Another disadvantage of the Internet is being exposed to the world of computer *viruses*. A computer virus can corrupt the files on your computer or delete them altogether. The only way to protect your computer from this sort of abuse is to install a security system, such as a virus scanner or firewall and keep it updated.

Be very wary of downloading programs onto your computer from sites you don't know much about, as they can contain viruses and spyware files.

Phone Calls on the Internet

Did you know you can make very affordable phone calls over the Internet? This is a huge benefit for anyone calling friends or family regularly. Businesses have realised the benefits too and they are making great savings on their phone bills. The person you 'call' doesn't need to be connected to a computer, you can call directly to their home phone! All you need is access to the Internet and a microphone connected to the sound card in your computer.

There are many businesses offering this technology, so if you'd like to learn more, just type VOIP (which stands for 'Voice Over Internet Protocol') into a search engine to find one suitable for you.

Legitimate Business and Information

Although it is necessary to stay cautious, the majority of information on the Internet is written legitimately and volumes of useful information can be obtained very quickly.

Small businesses are started every day with the Internet being their only shop front. Big businesses are using the Internet to streamline some of their functions. Academics and writers use the Internet to publish their work. As long as you have a means to verify what you receive from the Internet, you can be confident that it contains legitimate information.

The Internet is a very interesting, fun and opportunity-filled tool that, if used wisely, can be of great benefit to students at University. The usefulness of the tool far outweighs the pitfalls. Treat the Internet with respect and caution and you will find you have a wealth of information at your fingertips.

Summary

- *The Internet is an easily accessible tool containing vast amounts of information*
- *Information found on the Internet should always be verified*
- *Use a security system to protect your computer and keep it updated*

Have An Outlet

29

An outlet is an activity you do regularly for enjoyment. This could be playing music, playing a sport, creating art, swimming, running, walking on the beach or anything that takes your mind away from your studies and allows you to return refreshed. It is an activity that relaxes and refreshes your mind so you can get back to studying efficiently. If you don't have one, find an outlet that suits you and use it regularly.

Having an outlet can be very rewarding and should not be considered a waste of time. Using the outlet specifically as it is intended can be more beneficial than spending hours trying to study. If your mind is not in the mood for study, or if you are mentally tired, you might as well be doing something you enjoy. Trying to study when you are not functioning efficiently only means you'll take longer than you should and to a lower standard, so you may have to do it all over again later anyway.

When I was studying at University, my outlets were swimming, rock climbing, trampolining and jogging along the beach. My peers used to ask me how I could get all my homework done when I spent so much time down at the sports facilities. My answer to that was easy. If I allowed myself to spend an hour in the pool or gym before I went to the library to study or do an assignment, I was waking up my body and refreshing my mind so I could re-focus on what I had to do. I found nothing more unproductive than sitting down to do work when I didn't want to be there or if I was mentally tired. I would only do around 10 minutes of productive work for every half hour I was there.

I planned when I was going to do study and when I was going to use my outlet to refresh my mind. I allowed myself to spend time doing the things I enjoyed and I used my outlet as a reward by saying, 'If I can get this all done in the next hour, I will have enough time to go and have a swim before I go home this afternoon'. Luckily, I also had a couple of friends who used the same sort of rewards for themselves and we often challenged each other to a game of squash or table tennis before we went to the library to work on assignments.

If sport is not what you enjoy doing, it makes no difference. What matters is that you have something you can call your outlet. Something that you enjoy doing enough to use to refresh and reward yourself. Just be wary that your outlet does not make you more tired mentally. For me, watching television is the opposite of an outlet because it makes me tired mentally. Surfing the Internet is the same and so too is reading to an extent. Don't get me wrong – I love reading and try to read for at least half an hour every night before I go to sleep. However, as reading eventually makes me tired, it would be the worst thing for me to do before I tried to do a couple of hours of intense study.

Funnily enough, now that I am working, my outlet is gymnastics. Try to imagine a 35 year old gymnast and you will understand how much I enjoy it. Most people my age would not consider attempting what I do on bars, beam, vault and floor. Maybe I'm still a child at heart.

I get so much enjoyment from gymnastics that I look forward to it all week. It is a mentally and physically tough sport. When I drive home from work some nights, it's the last thing I feel like doing. Yet, when I arrive and begin my program, I soon feel much more alive – I can switch my mind off my work and just enjoy the challenges my coach throws at me.

I always loved gymnastics when I was young and never thought I would ever get back into it again after I stopped at age 14. After I had my two children, I was looking for a sport to get immersed in, as I was lacking an outlet and that frustrated me. When I took my 3-year-old daughter to gymnastics for the first time, I was sitting there watching her and thinking, 'I wish I could be doing that again'. I half jokingly asked the instructor how old their oldest student was. She said '16'. I then said, 'How would you feel if someone twice that age wanted to start?' She said 'Who, *you?*' and I said 'Yes me!' and from then on, I have never looked back.

(Photos courtesy of Gymnastics Australia, taken by Delly Carr, Sporthoot).

Figure 3: My outlet is gymnastics and my inspiration is Oxana Chusovitina, shown here winning the silver medal on vault at the 2005 World Gymnastics Championships in Melbourne at the age of 30. I was privileged to be able to volunteer at the Championships and watch Oxana train and then win this medal.

Summary

- *Choose an outlet that refreshes your mind and body*
- *Make time to attend your outlet on a weekly basis*
- *Use your outlet as a reward when you complete goals*

Student Loans

30

The cost of education varies dramatically between countries and campuses. Some courses cost very little, if anything while others can cost hundreds of thousands of dollars. If you don't have the money in the bank before you start your course, you have two mainstream alternatives.

1. You can apply for a scholarship and have someone else pay for part, if not all of your study costs or

2. You can use a loan to fund part or all of it. This loan is normally payable in small increments over a long time, which may be deferred to start at a later date.

Obtaining a Loan

There are many student loans available, which can be obtained through the University, the government, a private lending company or a bank. Depending on your parents' or family's finances, you could also ask them for a partial loan to reduce the amount you need to borrow from an outside party.

No matter whom you obtain the loan from, it is important to understand fully the responsibilities and conditions attached to it. Normally, whatever you borrow, you must pay back, at some stage. It would be very irresponsible and dangerous in the long-term to dismiss the gravity of the act of borrowing money – especially from family. If you don't pay outside parties back under the terms of your loan, they may have the right to sell your possessions and your credit rating can be affected. If you default with a family member or a friend, you may lose your entire relationship with that person.

Terms and Conditions

Conditions, fees, interest rates and terms vary greatly between loans. It is very important that you understand each of these factors *before* you sign up for any loan, so you are aware of what and when you will have to start paying. Once a loan is signed and accepted from the lender, it is usually very difficult to change the conditions. Not having read the fine print is no excuse for defaulting on a loan. Many people fail to read the fine print and find themselves paying dearly for it.

Always check that the interest rate stated is the yearly interest rate

and not a monthly or weekly interest rate.

In terms of affordability, a low interest rate and long-term loan should have smaller repayments. Set up fees, ongoing fees and loan features however are also important factors to consider. A very expensive loan can be camouflaged behind one with a very low interest rate if it has high set up and ongoing fees. Early termination fees are also a consideration if you intend to pay your loan out before the final payment is due. Some lending institutions penalise this type of payout as they lose part of the interest they expected from the loan.

The conditions of a loan can vary greatly. Some loans don't require any repayments until your income reaches a certain level, which may not be until you have left University and started your career. Others require repayments to be made immediately. Whatever the conditions are, you should insist on being kept informed about how much you owe and when your payments are due. Organise with your lender that they send statements to you, at least every 3 months.

Interest Rates

Interest rates and the length of time you have to pay back the loan (the loan term), have a great impact on your repayments and the amount of money you have to pay back in total. Some lenders offer a 'honeymoon period', where the initial interest rate is lower than a normal rate. Be wary of these deals however, as the interest rate can go up above a normal rate after the 'honeymoon period' is over. Check and re-check your sums to be sure you are getting a good deal.

The tables below show you how these factors affect a loan for annual interest rates of between 0% and 14% and a loan term of between 1 and 30 years.

This table assumes the typical case of the loan interest being calculated daily and the repayments being paid monthly in arrears (at the end of each month). If your loan has a monthly interest rate – just multiply it by 12 to get the annual interest rate.

	Annual Interest Rate														
	0%	1%	2%	3%	4%	5%	6%	7%	8%	9%	10%	11%	12%	13%	14%
1	833.33	837.85	842.39	846.94	851.50	856.07	860.66	865.27	869.88	874.51	879.16	883.82	888.49	893.17	897.87
2	416.67	421.02	425.40	429.81	434.25	438.71	443.21	447.73	452.27	456.85	461.45	466.08	470.73	475.42	480.13
3	277.78	282.08	286.43	290.81	295.24	299.71	304.22	308.77	313.36	318.00	322.67	327.39	332.14	336.94	341.78
4	208.33	212.61	216.95	221.34	225.79	230.29	234.85	239.46	244.13	248.85	253.63	258.46	263.34	268.27	273.26
5	166.67	170.94	175.28	179.69	184.17	188.71	193.33	198.01	202.76	207.58	212.47	217.42	222.44	227.53	232.68
6	138.89	143.16	147.50	151.94	156.45	161.05	165.73	170.49	175.33	180.26	185.26	190.34	195.50	200.74	206.06
7	119.05	123.31	127.67	132.13	136.69	141.34	146.09	150.93	155.86	160.89	166.01	171.22	176.53	181.92	187.40
8	104.17	108.43	112.81	117.30	121.89	126.60	131.41	136.34	141.37	146.50	151.74	157.08	162.53	168.07	173.72
9	92.59	96.86	101.25	105.77	110.41	115.17	120.06	125.06	130.19	135.43	140.79	146.26	151.84	157.54	163.34
10	83.33	87.60	92.01	96.56	101.25	106.07	111.02	116.11	121.33	126.68	132.15	137.75	143.47	149.31	155.27
11	75.76	80.03	84.46	89.04	93.77	98.64	103.67	108.84	114.15	119.61	125.20	130.92	136.78	142.76	148.87
12	69.44	73.72	78.17	82.78	87.55	92.49	97.59	102.84	108.25	113.80	119.51	125.36	131.34	137.46	143.71
13	64.10	68.39	72.85	77.49	82.31	87.31	92.47	97.81	103.31	108.97	114.78	120.75	126.87	133.12	139.51
14	59.52	63.81	68.29	72.97	77.83	82.89	88.12	93.54	99.13	104.89	110.82	116.91	123.14	129.53	136.05
15	55.56	59.85	64.35	69.06	73.97	79.08	84.39	89.88	95.57	101.43	107.46	113.66	120.02	126.52	133.17
16	52.08	56.38	60.90	65.64	70.60	75.77	81.14	86.72	92.49	98.45	104.59	110.90	117.37	124.00	130.77
17	49.02	53.32	57.86	62.64	67.64	72.87	78.31	83.97	89.83	95.88	102.12	108.54	115.12	121.86	128.75
18	46.30	50.61	55.17	59.97	65.02	70.30	75.82	81.55	87.50	93.64	99.98	106.50	113.20	120.04	127.04
19	43.86	48.18	52.76	57.59	62.69	68.03	73.61	79.42	85.45	91.69	98.13	104.75	111.54	118.49	125.59
20	41.67	45.99	50.59	55.46	60.60	66.00	71.64	77.53	83.64	89.97	96.50	103.22	110.11	117.16	124.35
21	39.68	44.01	48.63	53.53	58.72	64.17	69.89	75.85	82.04	88.46	95.08	101.89	108.87	116.01	123.30
22	37.88	42.21	46.85	51.79	57.02	62.53	68.31	74.34	80.62	87.12	93.82	100.72	107.79	115.02	122.39
23	36.23	40.57	45.23	50.20	55.48	61.04	66.88	72.99	79.35	85.93	92.72	99.70	106.86	114.17	121.62
24	34.72	39.07	43.75	48.75	54.07	59.69	65.60	71.78	78.21	84.87	91.74	98.80	106.04	113.43	120.95
25	33.33	37.69	42.39	47.42	52.78	58.46	64.43	70.68	77.18	83.92	90.87	98.01	105.32	112.78	120.38
26	32.05	36.41	41.13	46.20	51.60	57.33	63.37	69.68	76.26	83.07	90.10	97.31	104.70	112.22	119.88
27	30.86	35.23	39.97	45.07	50.52	56.30	62.40	68.78	75.43	82.31	89.41	96.70	104.14	111.74	119.45
28	29.76	34.14	38.89	44.03	49.52	55.36	61.51	67.96	74.68	81.63	88.80	96.15	103.66	111.31	119.08
29	28.74	33.12	37.89	43.06	48.60	54.49	60.70	67.21	73.99	81.02	88.25	95.66	103.24	110.94	118.76
30	27.78	32.16	36.96	42.16	47.74	53.68	59.96	66.53	73.38	80.46	87.76	95.23	102.86	110.62	118.49

Number of Years For Loan (Term)

Table 1: Calculated Monthly Loan Repayments if you Borrow $10,000. Assumes no ongoing fees.

If you had a $10,000.00 loan to be paid back in 5 years with an annual interest rate of 10%, you would have to pay $212.47 per month, for 60 months.

Total Amount Paid

This table shows the *total amount* you will pay over the term of the loan. You can see how the interest rate has little effect over a short-term loan, yet if the loan has a much longer term, you could be paying many times the initial amount.

	Annual Interest Rate														
	0%	1%	2%	3%	4%	5%	6%	7%	8%	9%	10%	11%	12%	13%	14%
1	10,000	10,054	10,109	10,163	10,218	10,273	10,328	10,383	10,439	10,494	10,550	10,606	10,662	10,718	10,774
2	10,000	10,104	10,210	10,315	10,422	10,529	10,637	10,745	10,855	10,964	11,075	11,186	11,298	11,410	11,523
3	10,000	10,155	10,311	10,469	10,629	10,790	10,952	11,116	11,281	11,448	11,616	11,786	11,957	12,130	12,304
4	10,000	10,205	10,414	10,624	10,838	11,054	11,273	11,494	11,718	11,945	12,174	12,406	12,640	12,877	13,117
5	10,000	10,256	10,517	10,781	11,050	11,323	11,600	11,881	12,166	12,455	12,748	13,045	13,347	13,652	13,961
6	10,000	10,307	10,620	10,939	11,265	11,596	11,932	12,275	12,624	12,978	13,339	13,705	14,076	14,453	14,836
7	10,000	10,358	10,725	11,099	11,482	11,872	12,271	12,678	13,092	13,515	13,945	14,383	14,828	15,281	15,742
8	10,000	10,409	10,830	11,260	11,702	12,154	12,616	13,088	13,571	14,064	14,567	15,080	15,603	16,135	16,677
9	10,000	10,461	10,935	11,423	11,924	12,439	12,966	13,507	14,060	14,626	15,205	15,796	16,399	17,014	17,640
10	10,000	10,512	11,042	11,587	12,149	12,728	13,322	13,933	14,559	15,201	15,858	16,530	17,217	17,917	18,632
11	10,000	10,564	11,149	11,753	12,377	13,021	13,684	14,367	15,068	15,788	16,526	17,282	18,055	18,844	19,650
12	10,000	10,616	11,256	11,920	12,608	13,318	14,052	14,809	15,587	16,388	17,209	18,051	18,913	19,795	20,695
13	10,000	10,668	11,365	12,089	12,841	13,620	14,426	15,258	16,116	16,999	17,906	18,837	19,791	20,767	21,764
14	10,000	10,720	11,474	12,259	13,076	13,925	14,805	15,715	16,654	17,622	18,618	19,640	20,688	21,760	22,856
15	10,000	10,773	11,583	12,430	13,314	14,234	15,189	16,179	17,202	18,257	19,343	20,459	21,603	22,774	23,971
16	10,000	10,825	11,693	12,604	13,555	14,547	15,580	16,650	17,759	18,903	20,081	21,293	22,536	23,808	25,108
17	10,000	10,878	11,804	12,778	13,798	14,865	15,975	17,129	18,324	19,560	20,833	22,142	23,485	24,860	26,265
18	10,000	10,931	11,916	12,954	14,044	15,186	16,376	17,615	18,899	20,227	21,597	23,005	24,450	25,929	27,440
19	10,000	10,984	12,028	13,131	14,293	15,510	16,783	18,108	19,483	20,905	22,373	23,882	25,431	27,016	28,634
20	10,000	11,037	12,141	13,310	14,544	15,839	17,194	18,607	20,075	21,593	23,161	24,773	26,426	28,118	29,844
21	10,000	11,091	12,255	13,491	14,797	16,171	17,611	19,113	20,675	22,291	23,960	25,676	27,435	29,235	31,071
22	10,000	11,144	12,369	13,672	15,053	16,507	18,033	19,626	21,283	22,999	24,770	26,591	28,458	30,366	32,312
23	10,000	11,198	12,484	13,856	15,311	16,847	18,460	20,146	21,899	23,716	25,590	27,517	29,492	31,510	33,566
24	10,000	11,252	12,599	14,040	15,572	17,191	18,892	20,671	22,523	24,442	26,421	28,455	30,539	32,667	34,834
25	10,000	11,306	12,716	14,226	15,835	17,538	19,329	21,203	23,154	25,176	27,261	29,403	31,597	33,835	36,113
26	10,000	11,360	12,832	14,414	16,101	17,888	19,771	21,741	23,793	25,919	28,110	30,362	32,665	35,014	37,403
27	10,000	11,415	12,950	14,603	16,369	18,242	20,217	22,285	24,439	26,669	28,969	31,329	33,743	36,203	38,703
28	10,000	11,469	13,068	14,793	16,639	18,600	20,668	22,835	25,091	27,428	29,835	32,306	34,830	37,401	40,012
29	10,000	11,524	13,187	14,985	16,912	18,961	21,124	23,390	25,750	28,193	30,710	33,291	35,926	38,608	41,330
30	10,000	11,579	13,306	15,178	17,187	19,326	21,584	23,951	26,416	28,966	31,593	34,284	37,030	39,823	42,655

(Left axis label: Number of Years For Loan (Term))

Table 2 : Total Loan Payments if you Borrow $10,000 and Pay Off the Agreed Monthly Payment. Assumes no ongoing fees.

If you had a $10,000.00 loan to be paid back in 5 years with an annual interest rate of 10%, you would have to pay $212.47 per month, for 60 months and you would pay back a total of $12,748.20.

Extra Payments

Extra payments are always a wise investment if you have the cash available. You will pay off your loan quicker, if you simply repay a bit extra each month. Always check with your lender to make sure they don't penalise you for making extra payments.

Compare the number of years taken to pay the loan with the original loan term.

		Annual Interest Rate													
	0%	1%	2%	3%	4%	5%	6%	7%	8%	9%	10%	11%	12%	13%	14%
1	1	1	1	1	1	1	1	1	1	1	1	1	1	1	1
2	2	2	2	2	2	2	2	2	2	2	2	2	2	2	2
3	3	3	3	3	3	3	3	3	3	3	3	3	3	3	3
4	4	4	4	4	4	4	4	4	4	4	4	4	4	4	4
5	5	5	5	5	5	5	5	5	5	5	5	5	5	5	5
6	6	6	6	6	6	6	6	6	6	6	6	6	6	6	6
7	6	6	6	6	6	6	6	6	6	6	6	6	6	6	6
8	7	7	7	7	7	7	7	7	7	7	7	7	7	7	7
9	8	8	8	8	8	8	8	8	8	8	8	8	8	8	8
10	9	9	9	9	9	9	9	9	9	9	9	9	9	9	9
11	10	10	10	10	10	10	10	10	10	10	10	10	10	10	10
12	10	10	10	10	10	10	10	10	10	10	10	10	10	10	10
13	11	11	11	11	11	11	11	11	11	11	11	11	11	11	11
14	12	12	12	12	12	12	12	12	12	12	12	12	12	12	12
15	13	13	13	13	13	13	13	13	13	12	12	12	12	12	12
16	13	13	13	13	13	13	13	13	13	13	13	13	13	13	13
17	14	14	14	14	14	14	14	14	14	14	14	14	13	13	13
18	15	15	15	15	15	15	15	15	14	14	14	14	14	14	14
19	15	15	15	15	15	15	15	15	15	15	15	15	14	14	14
20	16	16	16	16	16	16	16	16	16	15	15	15	15	15	15
21	17	17	17	17	17	17	16	16	16	16	16	16	15	15	15
22	17	17	17	17	17	17	17	17	17	17	16	16	16	16	15
23	18	18	18	18	18	18	18	17	17	17	17	16	16	16	16
24	19	19	19	18	18	18	18	18	18	17	17	17	17	16	16
25	19	19	19	19	19	19	19	18	18	18	18	17	17	17	16
26	20	20	20	20	20	19	19	19	19	18	18	18	17	17	16
27	20	20	20	20	20	20	20	19	19	19	18	18	17	17	17
28	21	21	21	21	21	20	20	20	19	19	19	18	18	17	17
29	22	21	21	21	21	21	21	20	20	19	19	18	18	17	17
30	22	22	22	22	22	21	21	21	20	20	19	19	18	18	17

Original Number of Years For Loan (Term)

Table 3 : Number of Years Taken to Pay Off a $10,000 Loan if You Pay $10 Extra Per Month. Assumes no ongoing fees.

For example, if you have a $10,000.00 loan with a loan term of 20 years and an annual interest rate of 10%, you would take 20 years to pay it off if you paid the agreed monthly payment of $96.50. (See Table 1) However, if you paid an *extra* $10.00 per month, or a *total* of $106.50 per month, you would pay out your loan in just 15 years.

Higher Extra Payments

This Table shows the effect on the term of your loan if you pay an extra $20 per month. Notice how over a long-term loan, with a high interest rate, the loan can be paid in less than half the original expected time, with only a small increase in the monthly payment.

	Annual Interest Rate														
	0%	1%	2%	3%	4%	5%	6%	7%	8%	9%	10%	11%	12%	13%	14%
1	1	1	1	1	1	1	1	1	1	1	1	1	1	1	1
2	2	2	2	2	2	2	2	2	2	2	2	2	2	2	2
3	3	3	3	3	3	3	3	3	3	3	3	3	3	3	3
4	4	4	4	4	4	4	4	4	4	4	4	4	4	4	4
5	4	4	4	4	4	4	4	4	4	4	4	4	4	4	4
6	5	5	5	5	5	5	5	5	5	5	5	5	5	5	5
7	6	6	6	6	6	6	6	6	6	6	6	6	6	6	6
8	7	7	7	7	7	7	7	7	7	7	7	7	7	7	7
9	7	7	7	7	7	7	7	7	7	7	7	7	7	7	7
10	8	8	8	8	8	8	8	8	8	8	8	8	8	8	8
11	9	9	9	9	9	9	9	9	9	9	9	9	9	8	8
12	9	9	9	9	9	9	9	9	9	9	9	9	9	9	9
13	10	10	10	10	10	10	10	10	10	10	10	10	10	10	9
14	10	10	10	10	10	10	10	10	10	10	10	10	10	10	10
15	11	11	11	11	11	11	11	11	11	11	11	11	10	10	10
16	12	12	12	12	11	11	11	11	11	11	11	11	11	11	11
17	12	12	12	12	12	12	12	12	12	12	12	11	11	11	11
18	13	13	13	13	12	12	12	12	12	12	12	12	12	11	11
19	13	13	13	13	13	13	13	13	13	12	12	12	12	12	12
20	14	14	13	13	13	13	13	13	13	13	13	12	12	12	12
21	14	14	14	14	14	14	14	13	13	13	13	13	13	12	12
22	14	14	14	14	14	14	14	14	14	13	13	13	13	13	12
23	15	15	15	15	15	14	14	14	14	14	14	13	13	13	12
24	15	15	15	15	15	15	15	14	14	14	14	13	13	13	13
25	16	16	16	15	15	15	15	15	15	14	14	14	13	13	13
26	16	16	16	16	16	16	15	15	15	15	14	14	14	13	13
27	16	16	16	16	16	16	15	15	15	15	14	14	14	13	13
28	17	17	17	17	16	16	16	16	15	15	15	14	14	13	13
29	17	17	17	17	17	16	16	16	15	15	15	14	14	14	13
30	17	17	17	17	17	17	16	16	16	15	15	14	14	14	13

Table 4 : Number of Years Taken to Pay Off a $10,000 Loan if You Pay an Extra $20 Per Month. Assumes no ongoing fees.

For example, if you have a $10,000.00 loan with a loan term of 20 years and an annual interest rate of 12%, you would take 20 years to pay it off if you paid the agreed monthly payment of $110.11. (See Table 1) However, if you paid an *extra* $20.00 per month, or a *total* of $130.11 per month, you would pay out your loan in just 12 years.

Criteria

All lenders have specific *criteria* that borrowers must comply with before they will lend any money. If you want to apply for a loan, make sure you can fill in the application form, in a clear, neat and complete manner. Many people have their applications rejected simply because they have not been able to complete the application form to the bank's satisfaction. It gives the lender the impression you don't really care about the money you are applying for and that you are not capable of performing a simple task. They might be asking themselves, *if this person can't fill in a form properly, will they take the loan seriously and keep up their repayments?*

Lenders look at your three C's when deciding whether or not to lend you money.

Collateral: The security you can offer against the loan. This may be your car, boat, house or anything else you own that the bank can sell if you don't repay your loan. The value of the collateral usually has to equal a good proportion of the loan amount. This may not apply to a student loan as most students have little collateral. Check with the banks on what they require as each institution is different.

Cash-flow: The amount of money you earn compared to the amount of money you spend. They need to know that there is sufficient money left over each month to cover their loan repayments. Banks are usually quite conservative with these calculations to make sure you don't over commit yourself by taking out a loan that you will find hard to pay back.

Character: They will usually want to find out a little bit about you. The more they know about you and the lifestyle you lead, the more they will be able to judge whether or not you will be a good risk as a borrower.

It is always handy to have an up-to-date spreadsheet that keeps track of all your income and expenses so you will know whether or not you can afford something before you buy it. There is a simple but useful spreadsheet available on the University Wisdom website at

www.universitywisdom.com/loans

This spreadsheet simply calculates your surplus income, or the income you could use to service a loan. If your surplus amount is negative, you are spending more than you are earning and you have no funds available to service a loan. In this case, you would be very unlikely to be offered a loan, except perhaps one at a very high interest rate. (See Chapter 15 on Financial Budgets).

If however you do have positive surplus funds available each month, you may have some loan capacity. The amount a bank may lend you will depend on your three C's as well as the formula they use to calculate your borrowing capacity and any credit history you have.

Banks use many different formulas, so not all banks will give you the same answer or the same amount, if any. Always shop around and find the loan that best suits you. If the first bank says no, that doesn't mean they all will. Conditions and fees will vary, making shopping around even more important.

For practice, fill in the application form on the next page. It gives you an indication of the sorts of questions a lender might ask. Make sure a bank form doesn't end up in a mess with rips, folds or coffee stains all over it. These factors detract from the lender's initial impression of you. Use the same pen for all the sections and be precise about any numbers you write down. If you don't have all the information to fill in the practice form, make time to find it and then finish it later. This information should be kept in a safe place, where you can access it whenever you need it.

UNIVERSITY WISDOM

Practice Finance

1234 Lending Road, Nowhere.
Tel: 12345678 Fax: 12345678 Mob: 12345678

PRACTICE APPLICATION FOR FINANCE

NAME OF APPLICANT: _____

ADDRESS: _____

TELEPHONE: _____ FAX: _____ MOBILE: _____

OCCUPATION: _____ SINCE: _____

PROPOSAL: (What do you want the money for)

_____
_____
_____
_____

BACKGROUND: (Write down a bit about yourself)

_____
_____
_____
_____

FINANCIAL INFORMATION & COMMENTS: (Write down if you have ever had a loan before)

_____
_____
_____
_____

SECURITY OFFERED: (What do you own that the bank could sell if you can't pay off your loan)

_____
_____
_____
_____

GENERAL INFORMATION: (Tell them anything else about yourself that may help your application)

_____
_____
_____
_____

FUNDS WILL BE USED FOR: O Lease   O Asset Purchase

                            O Rental   O Other

STATEMENT OF FINANCIAL POSITION

Name of Applicant: _____

Assets	Value	Liabilities	Total Owing	Monthly Payments
Residence:	$	**Mortgage Loan**	$	$
Other Properties		**Other Mortgage Loans**		
1.	$	**1. Owing to**	$	$
2.	$	**2. Owing to**	$	$
Furniture/Fittings	$	**Personal Loans**	$	$
Motor Vehicles	$	**Lease/Hire Purchase**		
1.	$	**1.**	$	$
Cash on Hand/Bank	$	**Bank Overdraft Limit**	$	$
Investments		**Credit Card/s Limit**	$	$
1.Superannuation	$			
2.	$	**Unpaid Tax**	$	$
Other Assets (Details)	$	**Other Liabilities (Details)**	$	$
TOTAL ASSETS (1)	$	**TOTAL LIABILITIES (2)**	$	
NET SURPLUS (1)-(2)	$			

References (Who can the bank ring to verify your application)

Name	Phone Number	Relationship

Accountant: _____ **Contact:**_____ **Phone:**_____

Bank Name:_____ **Branch:**_____ **Since:**_____

Heath Insurer:_____ **Policy Type:**_____ **Policy No:**_____

Signed:_____ **Dated:**_____

You can download this practice form at www.universitywisdom.com/loans

Summary

● *Always understand the terms and conditions of any loan you agree to*

● *Make sure you will be able to meet your loan repayments comfortably*

● *Extra payments can reduce your loan term – always check for any penalties*

Scholarships

Availability

There are thousands of scholarships offered every year from numerous sources around the world. Some are specific to a course at a certain University. Some have very broad criteria and allow students to study anywhere in the world. Some scholarships offer students a fully funded degree. Others offer an amount of money to the student for one year of a course, or a monthly stipend throughout the whole course. Whatever course you are doing, there may well be funds available to help you.

Not all scholarships are academically based; so don't think only the brightest students have any hope of obtaining one. Your personality and commitment to complete the course may be just as important qualities. Some companies offer students scholarships as a way of enticing newly qualified recruits. For them, a student they know, who is easy to work with would be a prime target for a scholarship because they will already have some knowledge of the company by the time they graduate.

A scholarship is not something that will necessarily fall into your lap if you are a top grade student. In order to receive a scholarship, you have to apply. You need to search for a scholarship whose criteria you fulfil. You will need to fill in the application form by the due date and then and only then, will you be considered as a candidate for that scholarship.

Where to Find Them

There is usually a section at Universities totally dedicated to helping students get the information they need to apply for scholarships. This may be just a reference area where books are held listing the scholarships available around the world. It will then be up to you to search and apply for an appropriate scholarship.

It's important to remember that although the scholarship section at University should have a comprehensive list of scholarships available, it will not be exhaustive. This is because some local community groups set aside funds for miscellaneous activities. They may want to use some money for a good cause so they will be unlikely to restrict themselves to offering a scholarship for someone going to University - just in case something they feel more worthwhile comes up. If you live in a community where there is a fund-raising group, it might be worth approaching them with your goals and plans to see if there is anything they can do to help you.

When you approach someone with the hope of receiving a scholarship, avoid just asking for money. Have a list of your goals and plans and be prepared to talk about yourself for a while so the people involved can get to know you. Don't expect to get an answer immediately, as proposals to a fund-raising group usually have to go through a committee. You might be surprised by how these groups can help you even if they can't offer you money.

A great resource for finding scholarships is the Internet and there are many worthwhile websites to look at. If you are interested in getting a scholarship this way, have a look at the following addresses for some ideas:

http://www.ausaid.gov.au/scholar http://www.scholarship-page.com
http://www.colleges.com http://www.britishcouncil.org/

You can find more links to scholarships at www.universitywisdom.com/scholarships

As the Internet is not a verifiable source (See Chapter 28), be careful about giving away your personal information, including your email address. Before you apply for any scholarship online, do some research into the University, company or group first. If there are no contact details such as a phone number or an address (that you can write to or visit), then be very cautious about applying.

If you would like to pursue a scholarship, spend time looking for everything available to you well ahead of your course start date. Research the sources, the limits and the restrictions on the scholarships and be prepared for the fact that if you have one scholarship, it may well exclude you from obtaining any others. This is a logical and fair precaution to ensure that one person doesn't obtain more than their fair share, to the detriment of others.

Work Experience

Some scholarships offer students work experience during their course. This is an invaluable aspect of the offer, especially if the students are genuinely interested in what the company does. Any professional experience is a bonus, so the opportunity should be embraced. This gives the company a way of getting to know you and to test you in the work force. If they grow to like you through your scholarship, they may offer you a job well before you finish your course.

In the space below, write down some sources of scholarships you could pursue, at your earliest convenience. Write down some companies you might like to work for and contact them to see if they offer any scholarship programs.

_____

_____

_____

_____

_____

_____

_____

_____

_____

_____

_____

_____

_____

_____

Summary

- *There are thousands of scholarships offered to students all over the world*
- *You need to find a scholarship whose criteria you meet*
- *Make sure you apply for scholarships by the due date in order to be considered*

Getting Experience

Your Curriculum Vitae (CV) or Resume is a great asset that may carry you into many new and exciting jobs. It is a short document summarising your identity and the notable achievements and experiences you have gained to date. Your potential employers will compare your Resume with many others in order to decide who to interview. It will give them a lasting impression of you, so fill it with lots of interesting information.

Having work experience during your course is very worthwhile and will give you great insight into what you are studying and why. These experiences will give you the ability to construct an interesting Resume and provide topics of discussion with your potential employers during an interview.

As long as you are not out of pocket, try not to be too concerned about the pay you receive for experience as a student – no matter how little it seems at the time. If you are working and learning, think of it as free education! If you actually get paid to learn as well, you are miles in front and should count your blessings.

Your employer is giving you an opportunity to learn and improve your Resume, which could help you start your career. Of course, they are getting help in return so it is a win-win situation – as it should be. Not one potential employer has ever asked me how much I was paid for my summer-holiday work experiences. They have only ever been interested in *what I learnt* during those three months each year.

> I was so grateful to be getting experience in my chosen career that the money I was paid was just a bonus. Many of my friends found it hard to find relevant work and had to settle for a part-time job doing something unrelated to their studies. Yet, this was still good experience for them and if nothing else, taught them some of the aspects of how a business is run. I could never understand those who refused to work in a field that was not directly related to their course.

Some students feel cheated when they are employed, as they are not paid a full wage, or they don't get to do 'real work'. They may end up filing or doing tasks that no one else wants to do. However, as a student, you are not fully qualified, so you can't expect to be given the salary or responsibilities of a graduate. Simply networking with other professionals in your field is a priceless experience. You never know who will be looking to recruit when you graduate.

On the following pages, construct a brief Resume by filling in the blank spaces. Make sure the experiences you put down are truthful; no matter how trivial they sound. As you gain more experience, you will be able to update this brief summary and make a professional document out of it.

Your Resume is all about you. Be proud of it!

Summary

- *Having work experiences as a student will give you insight into different careers*
- *Work experience is just that – The pay is a bonus*
- *Your Resume will draw on all your experiences – Make the most of them*

Resume

Name :_____

Date of Birth :_____

Address :_____

Phone / Fax :_____

eMail :_____

Website:_____

Place Your

Photo Here

Academic History

_____

_____

_____

_____

_____

_____

_____

_____

_____

_____

_____

Academic Achievements

_____

_____

_____

_____

_____

_____

_____

_____

_____

_____

_____

_____

Work Experience

- _____

_____

_____

- _____

_____

_____

- _____

_____

_____

- _____

_____

_____

- _____

_____

_____

- _____

_____

_____

- _____

_____

_____

- _____

_____

_____

- _____

_____

_____

Achievements Outside School / University

Community Involvement

- _____
- _____
- _____
- _____
- _____

Sports and Hobbies

- _____
- _____
- _____
- _____
- _____

Goals

- _____
- _____
- _____
- _____
- _____

Referees	**1**	**2**
Name:	_____	_____
Company:	_____	_____
Position:	_____	_____
Address:	_____	_____
Phone / Fax:	_____	_____
eMail:	_____	_____
Website:	_____	_____

If you would like a copy of this resume template as a three-page document, just go to www.universitywisdom.com/resume and download it yourself.

PART 4

What may stop you?

Life's Limitations

Limitation is unfortunately a fact of life. No one has an infinite amount of time or boundless resources. Accepting this allows you to make good use of the time you have and opportunities that come your way. Particularly as a student at University, there will be limits on your time, what you read and how you manage your money.

Time

Time is a part of life that everyone is restricted by as we all only have 24 hours in a day.

Those who live in the make believe world of no limits blissfully slide through life doing whatever they feel like, or what everyone else is doing. They can waste precious time watching whatever comes onto the television or endless movies. They have little concept of time and the power it gives you to succeed. These people often wonder where their life went when they get old.

Efficient people are aware of the restriction of time and use as much of it as possible to move forward. They make conscious decisions about how they use their time and often give up the opportunity to do something everyone else is doing in preference to doing something they think is more important to them.

People who are diagnosed with a terminal illness are often heard saying – 'I'm going to really make good use of the time I have left'. They think more about what is important to them and strive to achieve certain goals before they go. So why does it take this tragic news to make us stop and think? Shouldn't we all be striving to make good use of the time we have left?

What we Read

Reading is a pastime that many people love, yet both time and the sheer volume of material available restricts *what we read*. There is more print material produced per day than anyone would ever be able to read in 24 hours.

Those who live in the make believe world of no limits are quite happy to read through pages and pages of material that is not useful to them. They read whatever comes into their view, like the gossip columns in the papers and magazines and the brochures that marketing companies put in their letter box. This cycle of information gathering never ends and is a typical time wasting exercise. These people tend to know a little bit about many things but seldom become a master of any.

Successful people however, choose to read what they find interesting, what they enjoy and what they need to read to learn. They choose *not* to read certain publications, as they are a distraction from what they choose to read. These people usually strive to become proficient in a subject, a skill or a hobby and they tend to read a lot about that.

Money

In order to be content and survive financially, we need to accept the limitation of money. As most parents have to explain to their children, 'money doesn't grow on trees' or 'spend your pocket money wisely'. We can all learn from that advice as adults; even the richest people in the world have to make decisions about how they spend and invest their money.

Those who live in the make believe world of no limits tend to shop on impulse without considering the real value of the products they buy. They can spend like there is no tomorrow and apply for credit with little concern for the future. They often live week to week on their salary and may have nothing left the day before they are paid again. They look for ways to spend their money and go down to a shopping mall to wander, later finding they have bought items they didn't need. Monthly bills come in as a shock and can often not be paid on time because they have not been budgeted for. They rarely have a savings or investment plan and have little after years of working. These people have no common sense when it comes to money and marketing companies love them. They are the 'easy' customers, who throw money at anything because they don't know what else to do with it.

Financially successful people, who understand the limits of money, are very choosy about their purchases and make sure they get value for money. They don't have a problem saying 'no' to a purchase, no matter what pressures are put on them to spend.

These people try to make their money *work for them* through investments and they often have financial goals in place. They keep track of what they spend and look at ways of reducing their costs. They work to a budget and anticipate their bills. They choose to buy products that improve in value over time, and minimise those that are worthless as soon as they come out of the shop. They are very wary of credit and only use it with consideration and caution. Usually, paying off high interest loans is their first priority. Most financially successful people however are willing to wait until they can afford the things they want and avoid high interest loans altogether.

By accepting that life is bounded by certain limitations, we are forced to make wise decisions.

Alternatively, we risk living in the make-believe world of no limitations. There, life may be fun and enjoyable but the lack of success at anything may lead to a very average existence where

- time to do what you dream about quickly runs out

- little knowledge about anything leads to boredom and

- no money for the comforts of life eventually drags the smile off your face.

Life imposes limitations on your ability to fulfil your goals and plans. By accepting the limits you have now and those you will have in the future, you may find yourself making wise decisions that can allow you to spend more time and effort on goals you'd really like to achieve. You will have more time to read and learn about a topic that fascinates you and by limiting the time and money you spend on trivial things, you may be opening the possibilities for your passions to an extent where the sky really is the only limit!

Summary

- *We are all limited by time and money*
- *Try to use what you have to its full potential by making wise decisions*
- *Reducing what you spend in one area allows you to spend more in another*

Accept Sacrifices

There are some things you probably won't be able to do whilst you are a student at University due to restricted finances, time and having study commitments. There will have to be sacrifices made. There are also many benefits of being a student and these should be taken full advantage of, such as cheaper travel, accommodation, bank loans and entertainment tickets. Find out about these discounts and offers early so you don't miss out on them.

While you are at University, try not to compare yourself with friends who go straight into a full-time job after they finish High School. They are likely to earn a good deal more than you and will have the flexibility to go out or relax in their spare time. You, on the other hand, may have study to do after University hours or you may have to work part-time to pay for your education.

These sacrifices you make while you are a University student are all *short-term*. Once you finish your degree and start working in the career of your choice, you should have more spare time and hopefully a regular income too.

Being happy with your career is far more important than the sacrifices you make while you are a University student. Money and lifestyle cannot compensate for the long-term stresses caused by making a bad career choice.

No one gets to go to University without having made a lot of sacrifices beforehand.

As the saying goes 'There is no gain without pain' – this is very true for University students.

Most people are in the work force a lot longer than they are at University. So rather than dwell on what you can't do as a student, utilise all the benefits and enjoy the lifestyle of a student while you can.

There are many wonderful aspects of being a student at University such as extended holidays, meeting new friends, experiencing intensive learning and having access to clubs and facilities. By putting time and effort into your chosen career, you are making possible a brighter, more enjoyable future for yourself and your family. Any short-term sacrifices should seem trivial in years to come.

Summary

- *Short-term sacrifices may have to be made while you are a student*
- *The benefits of a good career choice far outweigh the sacrifices*
- *Enjoy the unique lifestyle and benefits of being a student while you can*

The Roller Coaster

It's probably better to not start a course at all than to start it and never finish. Too many people regret later on in life not finishing the course they began because they wonder what life *might* have been like if they'd only pushed through the tough times and not given up. It is so easy to quit when things get tough so it is important to be prepared for a few ups and downs while you are studying. The Roller Coaster will most likely continue throughout your career as well. You may have some great times and some not so great times; some great jobs and some not so great jobs; some great managers and some not so great managers.

The truth is that all courses and professions have their ups and downs, their pros and cons. They all have good reasons to stay on and good reasons to quit. When your thoughts start wandering away from what you are doing and you start thinking about quitting, step back for a minute and think about why it is happening. Ask yourself what you did to prepare for the down side of The Roller Coaster. Secondly remind yourself how fortunate you are to be studying at University. Thirdly, think about and write down all the pros and cons of your course and what you would be doing in 5 years time if you continued, or if you quit.

> Sometimes I think that perhaps the 'grass would be greener' in a different profession. However, once I write down the pros and cons of what I am doing, I realise that I am in the best profession for me. I find this exercise allows me to re-focus my thoughts on the bigger picture, rather than get bogged down in any one problem I face on a day-to-day basis.

Most students go through some stage during their course when they want to quit. If you are prepared for that at the beginning, it won't come as such a surprise if it happens to you. You may also have more chance of getting through a problem when it surfaces, if you are prepared to experience some fluctuation in the way you feel about your course.

If your *mind* starts giving you warning signals by becoming negative, you need to acknowledge it and take notice. You may feel that you are not getting anywhere or the course may seem too hard or you are not happy with the course you got into because it wasn't your first choice. These thoughts can fester and cause much more anxiety than is necessary. You can use your *mind* to turn things around and take control again. Talk to someone about your concerns and work through any issues you have.

A University degree will not be given to you on a silver plate and, at times, you will have to work hard and long hours. You won't always understand everything or get the marks you think you deserve and there may be lecturers that you don't like. If you ever feel like quitting for any of these reasons, remember they are all part of a University degree and you won't be the first student to feel that way.

Try to think of all the positive aspects about being a University student. By doing that, you may be able to turn your mind around. Listen to friends who are positive about your course and try not to listen to those who give you plenty of reasons to take the easy option of quitting. Those same people probably won't be around you when and if you start regretting your decision.

Sometimes, *events and circumstances* can take over while you are at University and no matter how much you want to continue and do well, things beyond your control can influence your ability to perform. These types of events could be: parents getting ill and needing you to take care of them, having a wedding or a child while at University, having loved ones die or having to rely too heavily on a job. All these circumstances can result in your time and effort at University being compromised.

I breezed through my first two years of University, without a care in the world. I was studying Science and Engineering which is a fairly demanding five-year double degree. At the start of my third year, my boyfriend was killed in a tragic accident. I was 19 and he was 20. That was a very shocking experience and sent me spinning off course.

Within another couple of months, my Grandfather died. My father and I went to England for his funeral. I had been particularly close to him since I was young and had been to visit him many times. That was a very sad time for me.

The two weeks I had away from University meant that I missed lots of classes and I was really tired when I came home. Within another two months of our return, my other Grandfather died. My exam results that year were all over the place and far from the 80 to 90% I was used to. I had marks as low as 60% right up to a mark of 99%.

The head of my Engineering school asked me if everything was OK at home because he was worried that my marks had declined. When I told him what had happened that year, he arranged for me to be given special consideration for the end of year exams, which meant that if I needed more time and wanted to do them after the summer holidays, I could.

It surprised me how willing he was to help me get through. The following year I got myself back on track and tried to put the events of the previous year, which were totally out of my control, behind me. I focused on the years ahead and the prospect of going overseas with my studies, which made me more determined to pick up my grades again and move on.

When events like these happen, your normal pattern of studying, working and balancing life with sport and social activities is affected. No one can expect to go through a University course without any problems. The problems that affect us the most are the ones we least expect. Be prepared for some heartache, stress, problems and times when you will feel like quitting. If they don't come around then you are very lucky. If they do come, you may be better able to face them and work through them.

On the following page, write down as many pros and cons you can think of about the course you want to study. Be totally honest about both the positive and negative aspects. If you want to study a course and you think you will find it difficult, then write that down.

Imagine yourself going through each problem and having to deal with them one at a time. (For example: *If you think you will find the course difficult – picture yourself getting help*). Visualise yourself or your family benefiting from all the pros. *(For example: If you will enjoy a job you love – picture how happy it will make you)*. Always finish by re-reading your pros rather than your cons.

The Roller Coaster can affect anyone at Uni - All you have to do is be mentally prepared for the ride.

The Pros & Cons of my course are:

PROS (Positive Aspects)	CONS (Negative Aspects)

In 5 years time, I will be:	
If I continue my course	If I quit my course

Summary

- *There are pros and cons of every course and every career*
- *Some problems stem from the mind, while others are beyond your control*
- *Visualising yourself dealing with problems helps you to prepare for them*

Workers and Surfers vs Balance

Freedom and Diversity

Students come to University from all walks of life - some from the cities, others from small country towns. Some travel to University from their homes while others have to live away from home for the first time and may board at or near their campus. You may even find that some students have travelled from another country to attend University. It is a new but different experience for everyone starting their first year and a common impression students have initially is how different their life is compared to being at High School. All of a sudden, students can feel intimidated by their large new world of diversity and freedom. Finding individual balance can sometimes be a challenge.

> Starting my University degree after a year away, I noticed that many students who went straight to University from High School had a different attitude to me and many fell into one of two categories - 'Workers' or 'Surfers'.

'*Workers*' are those who believe that doing well at University is all that matters. They study hard at High School to get a place at University and then they study hard at University to get a well-paid, secure job at the end of it. All of this at the expense of their social life and real life experience. They become slaves to their work and often become 'burnt out' within a few years. They place too much emphasis on marks and being at the top of the class and not enough time experiencing the wider life challenges and fun that University offers.

> I met one student who had been the dux of her High School. She chose medicine because it was the hardest course to get into and she had the marks to get in. By the time she was in fifth year, she was suffering a mental breakdown. She realised she had done nothing with her life apart from study. She also realised that by the time she finished University she would be 24, at the prime of her life and she still would not have done anything for her own personal fulfilment. She knew that she would be going straight from University to a hospital where she would be facing everyone else's problems and that if she stayed in that profession, it would continue for the rest of her working life. She hadn't taken any sort of break and it was finally catching up with her. She knew she needed to take a more balanced approach to her studies and her University experience and perhaps take a year out to re-focus.

'*Surfers*' are those who believe they are stuck in yet another school for the next few years and they spend their time drifting, not really knowing what they are going to do at the end of it all. They have no direction, no passion and just live for the day. They don't focus on what they are taught or on what they are going to do once they have their 'piece of paper'. These students generally scrape through their exams, change course half way through, or drop out. They may have all the ability in the world but they lack direction.

Students who strive to become balanced professionals should be wary of falling into either the 'Worker' or 'Surfer' categories. 'Workers', who try so hard to do well, often burn out through over-work. They can eventually lose their desire to do well along with the passion they have for their career. 'Surfers', no matter how clever, can find it difficult to make a decision and therefore end up doing little with their talents. They may leave all their options open, by avoiding making a commitment to their course, but this can result in becoming a 'jack of all trades and master of none'.

Try to go to University with an open mind. Take on the challenges you face and be willing to change direction only if you find a *passion* that leads you somewhere different. Move on to the next phase of your life when you finish – you don't have to come out of University with a perfect score or the best-chosen subjects. What may be more important for you is that you come out of University with a balanced outlook on life and a qualification in something you are passionate about.

I recently went back to my own University, where I spent five years of my life and I couldn't believe how small it felt, even though the campus is over 100 acres in size. I felt so 'over' being a student there. I remembered how I felt when I drove myself there on my first day. I was over-awed by the size and feeling of freedom I found at that campus. 15 years later, it all felt so small and part of my past 'student life'. I felt like I knew every nook and cranny and when I watched the students, they seemed so young! I will always appreciate what I learnt at University, however my mind has definitely moved on.

Those who find balance in themselves and their lives at University can learn from their own mistakes and continue on with their head up high. They are unlikely to be either 'Workers' or 'Surfers'. They will move on and realise that only those who 'have a go', get anywhere in life.

Those who try to be perfect usually find fault in themselves and find it difficult to get over. On the other hand, those who are afraid of failure often find it hard to commit to anything and can end up being non-achievers. Some become eternal students, taking degree after degree, hoping to become correctly qualified in everything they are interested in. They can become so comfortable being a student they often feel scared of leaving University and of taking the next step in their career. Sadly, these people can become over qualified and very hard to employ. Balanced students look forward to their career and realise that being a University student is just one of the stepping-stones towards their career.

Finding the balance at University may take time. True success involves finding and maintaining this balance. You can't always expect to be top of the class in every subject every year. Nor can you expect to come out with perfect understanding about every subject you take. As the saying goes – 'Life is not a dress rehearsal'. Just try do your best, using the talent, resources and support you have and as many of the strategies in Part 3 of this book as you can. If you can do this, you will be well on your way to leaving University with clear direction towards your chosen career and a balanced outlook on life.

Summary

- *Workers and Surfers often make life hard for themselves unnecessarily*
- *Try to find and maintain balance as a University student*
- *Do your best with the talent, resources and support you have*

Exam Technique

Exams are an *inevitable part of assessment* so it is important for a University student to strive for good exam technique. Whether it is a practical or theoretical exam, your assessor will compare your results with all the other students to rank the class. Students with good exam technique are more likely to attain higher exam marks because they will be in tune with the requirements and will have lots of experience through practice exams before their own exam day.

Exams are designed to test the knowledge and skill of the student, within a limited time frame. Typically, average students will not finish all the tasks in an exam. They may get 80% of the questions done and 80% of what they attempt correct. A good student may finish all the questions but only get 80% of what they attempt correct. A top student will complete all the questions and get 100% of what they attempt correct.

Clarity

In exams, *every mark counts*, so it is important to be familiar with the correct layout expected for answers and the finer detail required for working out. For example: In a physics exam it is critical to include the correct *units* along with the answer, as an answer without units may only be worth half the marks of an answer with the right units. An answer of '5' may receive ½ a mark, even though the number has been calculated correctly, whereas an answer of '5 seconds' would result in a full mark.

The *layout* of your work should be readable and large enough to understand easily. A correct answer is worth very little if it cannot be read, or if the examiner has to spend too much time deciphering it. Be clear and obvious when you write answers. Think of the person who will have to mark your work and try to make it easy for them. Imagine having to assess 100 exams that are almost identical. By the time you had marked 20, you would be getting tired and more likely to mark down any that are messy or hard to read.

Having *familiarity* with past exams is one of the best methods of exam preparation available. If you can find past exam papers, you will be able to see the types of questions that are asked year after year. If these exams are not available at your University, there should be plenty of other past exams from other Universities freely available. Become familiar with these past exam papers early on in your course so you can study them as you learn the subject. They will be of great use to you when you need to study for your own exams.

The power of *visualisation* can dramatically increase your exam results with very little effort. No matter what course you do, there will probably be an element of memorising information required. Whether it is formulae, events and dates or famous quotes, writing them down on colourful posters and placing them on the walls around you, will help to ingrain them in your memory. Looking at the information for two or three minutes each day before you go to sleep and as soon as you wake up can make memorising so much easier, you may even remember it long after the posters come down.

I used this method through my final High School years and all the way through University. Each of my posters grouped similar formulae and each formula on a poster was written in a different colour. I had them all over my bedroom walls and ceiling. When I had to use one in an exam, I could visualise it as the 'blue' or 'green' formula and just wrote it down.

Some Universities allow the use of a 'cheat sheet' to be brought into an exam without penalty, as an aid for students. In the work force, we have textbooks available to us, so it is unnecessary to expect students to memorise everything. It is far more practical to examine the students' ability to *use* the information, rather than test their memorising skills. If a 'cheat sheet' is allowed in an exam, try to create it at least a month before. Be *familiar* with the sheet and test its suitability as you practise for the exam. A 'cheat sheet' written the night before may have all the information you need on it, but if you haven't practised with it and can't find what you need quickly, it may be more of a hindrance than a help.

Stay Calm

Good exam technique results in you completing the questions accurately in the time given. This requires you to control your stress levels and keep moving if a problem question is encountered. If you keep aware of the time available, you may be able to come back to these questions, after you finish those you can answer *correctly*. Always go into an exam expecting to find questions you can't answer so there are no crippling surprises. If a question looks easy, don't rush it and risk making a silly mistake - read it a second time and *make sure you get it right*.

Try not to take any notice of other students in an exam room. You should only be focusing on the paper in front of you and the time. A minute's distraction is a minute wasted.

Speed and Timing

If you are able to practise many past exams or questions, try using a clock and measure how long they take you to complete. If you finish early, use the time you have left to look through your paper for silly mistakes. If you get the answers all correct but take longer than the exam allows, you will need to work on your *speed* in order to improve. If you finish the exam within the time frame but get a low percentage correct, you will have to work on your *knowledge*. There is no point timing yourself with past exams until you have the knowledge to answer the questions correctly. Only then should you start honing your exam technique for speed.

With thorough preparation and good technique, exams become less daunting and higher marks can be achieved. Keep a positive attitude, know what is expected, control your stress to a healthy level and do as much as you can with the allocated time. Your results should then reflect your ability and you can be content to know you have done your best.

Summary

- *Write clear, readable, correct and complete answers*
- *Use visualisation as a tool for memorising information*
- *Once you have the knowledge, use past exams to hone your speed and timing*

Earning Money

38

You don't necessarily need a lot of money in the bank to study at University. There are loan schemes, scholarships and many part-time jobs offered around Universities, which are ideal for University students. Having to earn money while at University is very common and certainly achievable. What is needed is an open mind and good time management skills.

When I was at University, I was lucky enough to receive a scholarship, which paid for all my course fees as well as a limited number of textbooks. However, I still needed money for lunches and petrol as well as occasionally going out with friends. Most of my peers had a part-time job too. Very few had jobs that were directly related to their careers.

I was an engineering student and worked part-time as a swimming instructor. Another engineering student friend worked part-time in a pizza shop. An accounting friend worked part-time in a bookstore. We all found enjoyable low stress jobs that we could fit around our University timetables.

There are many opportunities to earn money while you are studying at University if you have an open mind. Although you may be studying to become a doctor or an engineer, the jobs available to you that will fit with your study timetable may be working in a video store or a theatre or sporting facility. Don't get hung up on what the job is; just see it as another stepping-stone - a means to fund your experience at University.

I really enjoyed working at the University swimming pool. I had always enjoyed swimming and racing myself so I got qualified as a swimming instructor and started teaching children on Saturday mornings. I then went on to learn Life Saving skills and became involved in my local Club. Within a year, I was teaching the Australian Bronze Medallion at the University. That led to me competing at the National level in Life Saving and representing my state, which I thoroughly enjoyed. I then became a squad instructor, teaching children how to race. I went on to become a "Poolie" or Lifeguard. I met lots of really nice people through that job and when I go back, even now, I still see old friends that I used to work with.

My other job while at University was being a tutor for High School students. I helped 2 or 3 students regularly each night in their homes after University was over. Again, it was a challenge and I enjoyed seeing students grow and do well at school. The students I found a pleasure to teach were those who knew they had some shortfalls and were willing to step back and learn something they may have not understood the year before. They were much more willing to listen and I put 100% into their lesson. Not so for those who thought they knew it all and blamed the teachers for not passing their exams. I knew they would find out their way, which was going to be the hard way.

This tutoring job became a great little business and paid for all my petrol and entertainment costs. It was a wonderful experience and gave me the inspiration to write this book, as my students often used to ask me what it was like to be at University.

Some students find they have to work too many hours to stay on top of their living costs. Their part-time job can have a negative impact on their study because they may miss classes or become too tired to concentrate in class. If you have higher than normal living costs while you are studying, try to reduce them so you can concentrate on your primary aim. Having a part-time job while studying at University is a great way to earn money, get business experience and meet new people. However, if you find you have to work too many hours, you must look at why your expenses are so high (See Chapter 15). With a realistic budget and good time management skills, you should be able to juggle working part-time as a University student.

If you know you will need to work part-time while studying as a University student, think about what jobs you could do either close to the University or close to where you will be living. Write down some companies you could contact or a small business (like tutoring) that you could start on your own. Be imaginative and think of things you might even enjoy! How about dressing up for children's parties or coaching a local sports group?

The jobs I could do while studying at University are:

_____

_____

_____

_____

Some companies that may offer this kind of work are:

_____

_____

_____

_____

The likely pay for this type of work would be _____ per hour.

I could work up to _____ hours during the week.

I could work up to _____ hours on the weekend.

Summary

- *A part-time job while studying can be very rewarding*
- *Be wary of the number of hours you work and travel during the week*
- *Try to find a job that is enjoyable for you and has flexible working hours*

Politics and Charities

It is at University that some students are first exposed to and become interested in politics and charity groups. Many Universities have branches of political parties and charities on campus. For some students, it can be a good outlet for youthful idealism. Debating and protesting can be a healthy means to voice one's opinion and is a good training ground for public speaking. Serving a charity can also be very worthwhile and satisfying. However, you will need to consider whether or not it is worth *your* time and effort to get involved, while you are a student at University.

At University, I steered clear of political parties and rallies because I already had enough to do and I didn't have the time or the energy to become involved in their activities. However, I did participate occasionally in fund-raising activities for charities.

You can get involved in politics at any time during your adult life. Once you finish your degree, you will have the benefit of a few years of maturity and may have formed your own opinions about issues, understanding more fully the complexities of the issues raised in the media.

If you find that you want to get involved in a group or charity during your University course, but don't have the time to volunteer yourself, look at supporting groups such as The Red Cross, Amnesty International, Engineers Without Borders, or one of the thousands of other groups making a real difference.

Australian Red Cross
www.redcross.org.au

amnesty international australia
www.amnesty.org.au

engineers
without borders
AUSTRALIA

www.ewb.org.au

Summary

- *Politics can be a good platform for public speaking and debating*
- *Consider your main aim when deciding whether or not to get involved*
- *There are many groups already working around the world that you can support*

Relationships

Most students at University experience at least one relationship during their degree. These may be mutually beneficial and great fun, a distraction and disaster or something in between. If both partners are aware of and are sympathetic to the stresses and demands of University, a relationship can be something to really look forward to. If not, one or both of the students may be torn between their commitment to their relationship and their studies.

There are many relationships at University that are not successful because the *relationship* becomes the primary aim of one or both the students. When this happens, it can make getting through classes, studying and exams more stressful and seem less important. When your top priorities get confused, the tug of war between them can become very destructive.

If student relationship issues are not resolved promptly,

the effects can be very negative and long lasting.

Be prepared for the confusion that may arise if you try to prioritise what you *have* to do before what you *want* to do. If you want your primary aim to remain passing your University degree, be wary of relationships if you know you will get very emotionally involved. Understand that exams are an emotional time for you as well.

If your partner wants to be with you for the majority of the time and gets upset if you choose study over going out, you may feel guilty and compromise your primary aim. If you try to do everything to please your partner and at the same time try to please your examination board, you may find yourself becoming totally exhausted. A relationship should ideally be positive and beneficial for both partners.

> I really appreciated Rob my husband-to-be while I was studying because of his stance on my education. He was willing to wait for me and not see me every day of the week because he knew how much my degree meant to me. He knew I needed time to study after class and on the weekends. He also realised that if he tried to make our relationship my primary focus, he would probably lose me altogether. He was willing to sacrifice some time together to make sure I completed my degree. I have always been grateful for that 'space', his selflessness and patience.

If a partner gives you a choice between your studies and your relationship, big decisions are needed *urgently*. Your partner may decide that your relationship is suffering because of *your* dedication to your studies. If this pressure is thrust upon you, it is important to re-visit your priority list and re-evaluate your primary aim. Only *you* can decide what to do and *you* have to take full responsibility for the decision you make. After all, it is your education and it is your relationship.

It is not surprising that a few students find themselves juggling their wedding plans while they are at University. Although some can manage the challenges and stress, many find it all too much. Planning a wedding is known to be one of the most stressful times in our lives and attending University can be also. If you are planning to organise your own wedding while you are at University, be careful not to over commit yourself.

> I was dating Rob in my final year of University. Thankfully, he decided to wait until after my exams to ask me to marry him. He understood how important my degree was to me and I really appreciated his attitude. This unselfish nature made me more fond of him, which is probably the opposite of what most partners would expect.

Just talking to your partner about how you are feeling will often solve a problem. It would be very difficult for anyone to fully understand the stresses of being a University student, if they have never been to University themselves. If they value your relationship, they will be willing to listen and accept the difficulties, without making you feel guilty.

Plan your time so you can spend some with a partner without compromising your studies. If your relationship starts to take over from your primary aim, talk about it with your partner and let him or her know what your priorities are. You will soon find out what his or her priorities are and what sacrifices he or she is willing to make for you – if any.

People's morals and values rarely change over time. If you don't like what you hear when you talk about your aims and goals, then think about living with that attitude for the rest of your life. Remember, there is no 'I' in the word TEAM and being a team is the basis of all good relationships.

Summary

- *Relationships should be mutually beneficial and enjoyable for both partners*
- *Talking to your partner can usually solve any problems that arise*
- *Consider your primary aim when dealing with a 'difficult' relationship*

Looking to the future

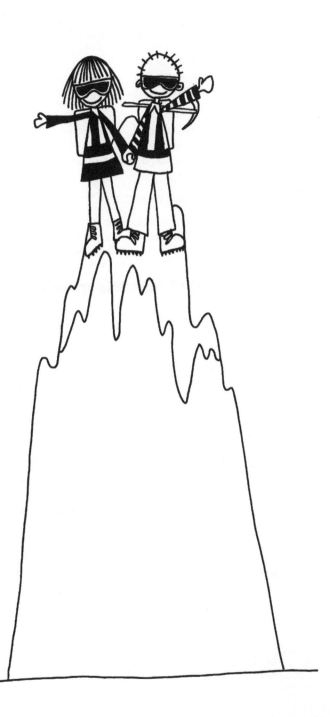

Follow Your Plan

The main strategies to being successful are simple and anyone can use them to reap great rewards. You don't need to be clever or wealthy, good looking or lucky. All you need is a good plan that you follow every day. For a small change in the way you work and organise your time, you can expect to see great improvements in the way you feel and the achievements you make.

Let's say that for each of the strategies given in Part 3 of *University Wisdom*, you need a 5% increase in effort. If you adopted just one of the strategies described, how much more successful do you think you could you be? For a 5% increase in effort, conservatively you might guess that you could be 5% more successful.

If however, you adopted two or more of the strategies, you could expect more than a 5% increase in your success. By increasing your effort just 5% in two or more different ways, a compounding effect may start to happen. Just like the formula for compound interest, the formula I have used for the graph below is

$$\text{Possible Performance} = (1 + 5\%)^{\text{Number of Strategies Adopted}}$$

This compounding effect due to adopting more than one strategy is shown figuratively below. Although there is no direct, measured comparison, this graph gives you an indication of the power of adopting more than one strategy to make your life more enjoyable and efficient.

The Power of Adopting more than one Strategy

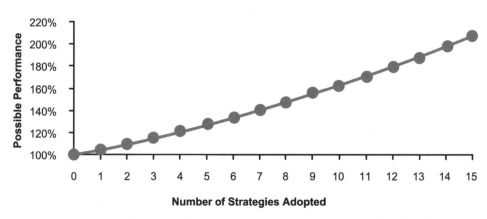

Figure 4: A figurative estimate of the possible Power of adopting more than one strategy described in Part 3.

It's easy isn't it! Just by adopting multiple strategies, having a plan and following it, the power of compounding can work for you, enabling you to make greater achievements.

Summary

● *Each strategy you adopt may require an extra effort of 5%*

● *Having a plan and following it will lead to your goals being achieved*

● *Using more than one strategy in your plan may create a compounding effect*

Investing Money

42

Most University students know little about the basics of investing. I know I didn't when I was studying and it was certainly not something my friends talked about. Most students save the money they need for rent, travel and food and spend the rest on clothes and going out. They tend to live week by week and don't even think about investing. They may save up for trips overseas or a car but general savings don't usually start until they are out of University and well into their first job.

> I lived like this for the first year of my University course. I was lucky that my sister had a job with an investment company and she introduced me to an investment plan. She opened my eyes to how I was wasting my money and how easy it would be for me to be investing. By the time I left University and was getting married, I had an account with over $7,000 in it!

Investing money is all about saving a small amount regularly, which over time, snowballs into a large amount. When you start investing, you can hardly see anything happening – it seems to grow so slowly that you wonder whether or not it is worth it. Over the long term however, the power of compounding interest kicks in and can make a huge difference to your balance.

If you invest $5,000 at the net return of 10%[3] per annum and let it sit there compounding and not adding to it, you would have $5,500 after one year, $8,052 after five years and $12,969 after 10 years. Just imagine if you let it sit for 45 years. You would then have a balance of $364,452! Keep in mind that inflation plays an important role in the devaluing of money and this must always be considered when you look at potential return from investments.

> When I started my savings plan, I was putting away approximately $76 per month. When I got my first statement, I was horrified to see that the money I could withdraw from it if I wanted to stop investing was less than what I had put in during the year! This was a really good reason to stay in the fund, as the units were not worth what I'd paid for them. I continued with this scheme for about 7 years and tracked every cent that went in from me and was earned in interest, as well as every cent that came out in fees.

> My initial goal was for the money to build up over time so that I could use it for my children's school fees. As I tracked the money and saw the fund producing poor results, I decided to take my money out. However, I wanted to make sure that I didn't lose any money. So, I waited until the portfolio was worth what I had put into it. That was a great lesson for me and it gave me some experience in investing by the time I left University.

Compound Interest

The most important concept of investing is that of *compounding* over time. There are many articles written in local papers and bank brochures, so it is not a concept that only savvy investors can understand. Someone interested in investing money should understand that investing doesn't happen overnight. Lottery happens overnight and only one in many millions win. *Anyone* can invest with a regular savings plan and a sound investment strategy. Turning small, frequent savings into a large portfolio over time is the fundamental concept of successful investing and saving through compounding.

The basic idea about compounding is that you earn interest on interest and assuming you have a net positive gain each year, your money grows at an ever increasing rate over time.

Tracking your investments is a great way to stay in touch with your investment goals. If you analyse your portfolio performance when you receive your statements, you can make wise decisions about the position of your money. Being uninterested in your investments can be a recipe for disaster as they could be losing money without you knowing. Before long, a bad investment can be worthless. Keeping interested and active in your investments can only give you the best chance of maximising your return.

"Compound Interest is the greatest Mathematical discovery of all time"
Albert Einstein

Shares

When a company is publically listed, their shares can be traded (bought and sold) on the share market. As a direct shareholder, you own a part of the company, albeit usually a very small percentage. Part of the profit made by the company during the year is then distributed to the shareholders either in the form of money or additional shares.

> I tracked some shares my parents bought me before I went to University. I was on a dividend reinvestment plan, which meant that any dividend I received was in the form of new shares instead of money in my bank account. I watched the shares with much interest and when the share price went right down, I thought if I had some money, I would buy some more. I didn't have any money at the time for investment, so I didn't make any purchases but the price is now well above where it was then, so I would have made a handsome return. My gut instinct was right but I wasn't in the position to do anything about it. That happens sometimes and it can be really frustrating.

If you are interested in learning about shares, there are some great sources of information on the Internet at: **www.asx.com.au   www.sanford.com.au   and   www.commsec.com**

These websites are mainly for Australian investors, however there are many other websites available for markets all over the world and a simple web engine search using the words "share market" would send you to the appropriate websites for your area. Remember, do a lot of research before you spend any money on shares.

Investment Research

If you are interested in learning about the basics of investment, I urge you to read the book "Rich Dad Poor Dad" by Robert Kyosaki. Robert explains some of the vital elements of investing in a really easy to understand way. He also explains that the most important element of investing is the time you allow it to mature. Of course, it's never too late to start investing. Yet, the earlier you start, the more financially secure you are likely to become and the sooner you may be able to give up your job, if you want to. You can find this book at: **www.richdad.com**

Credit Worthiness

The worst thing you can do when you are young is lose your credit rating, by not paying off your minimum monthly credit card payment on time or defaulting on one of your bills such as your rent, phone or electricity. If you get into short-term difficulty paying a bill, think about talking to your bank and letting them know what's going on. At least then they will know you are honest and may be more willing to help you through it. Best of all, be conservative with your money and don't ever let your savings get so low that you can't pay an unexpected bill or two.

It's important to understand the difference between good debt and bad debt, as debt is not always a bad thing. Good debt *makes* you money using other people's money while bad debt *loses* you money.

Good debt might be borrowing to buy a modest house or unit that helps pay itself off with the money it generates (through rent). The investment (the house or unit) is likely to be worth more over the long-term and should continue to generate money all the time you own it as long as it is rented. At the end of the loan, you have an asset worth more than the money you paid and it continues to make money for you.

Bad debt might be for a nice car that costs more than you really need to spend. The investment (the car) loses value over time and it generates no money to help pay for itself. At the end of the loan, you have something that is worth less than the money you have put into it and it still costs you money.

When you are more established in your career and have a few assets behind you, having a small amount of bad debt is OK. It's only when you are starting out that you should try to avoid it. Going from one bad debt to another is a bad habit to get into, especially if you are not investing at the same time. You might find yourself going backwards financially and wonder why life is such a struggle. Be very wary of credit card debt and keep your mind open if you hear about an investment that sounds deadly boring, like a savings plan - it might be the start of a very prosperous investment!

Depreciation and Appreciation

Depreciation is the way in which an item becomes less valuable over time. For example, a car might depreciate at the rate of 15% per year. A car worth $10,000 would only be worth $8,500 after one year and then $7,225 after two years.

Appreciation on the other hand is the way in which an item becomes more valuable over time. For example, a house might appreciate at a rate of 5% per year. A house worth $100,000 would be worth $105,000 after one year and then $110,250 after two years.

It's not hard to see why investors try to spend their money on items that appreciate rather than on those that depreciate.

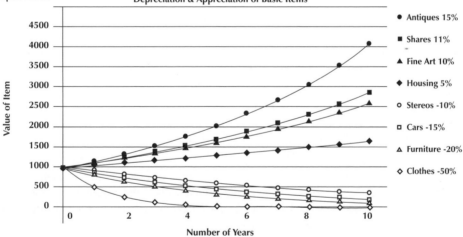

Figure 5: Current average appreciation rates for basic items. Negative appreciation is the same as depreciation. Various sources publically available on the Internet[4].

Summary

- *Investment and saving takes time and commitment*
- *Compounding allows interest or benefits to accumulate*
- *A good Credit Rating is a valuable asset – Protect yours*

Positive Cash Flow Property

Have you ever thought of owning a house or unit? If you are old enough to enter into a legal contract, then you may be able to buy property. On the other hand, real estate may be an asset you never want to own. This chapter is here merely to get you to *think* about the *practicalities* of owning it.

It may seem strange now, yet buying real estate early in life is a decision you may probably only appreciate after many years. Apart from the personal savings it forces you to make, owning real estate could make your plans and dreams achievable, once you build up a considerable amount of equity.

Most people who decide to buy real estate wonder why they didn't do it earlier. Real estate in the *long-term* generally increases in value and with the help of a *tenant* paying for the costs, ownership can become easier over time, as the property value and loan amount widens.

Real estate is an asset class banks will usually lend money against, because housing is a basic need for the majority of people and the value of the *mid price range real estate* is relatively stable. Banks may also lend against shares in listed companies and cash, however the leverage, (or the amount of money they will lend you over and above your deposit), against these two asset classes is generally lower.

If you like the idea of investing in real estate, don't rush out and buy the first house you find up for sale. There are many aspects of your finances, stability, lifestyle and ability to pay off a loan that will need to be considered before deciding whether or not to invest in the property market. It is also a must to get some professional advice.

A Few Basics

The price of housing at *each end* of the market generally *fluctuates* the most and novice investors should be very cautious when considering them. On the one hand, the very cheap (usually for good reason), remote houses can seem like a good buy, but often maintenance and repairs are costly and there are fewer people willing to live in these houses. On the other hand, the very chic, expensive houses can also have high maintenance costs and the rent often doesn't pay for the mortgage.

Buying real estate is a strategy that requires *knowledge* in order for it to be successful. You need to have knowledge about the housing market, the rental market, the economy and lending rates. You generally need to be able to prove to the bank that you can save money for a deposit, have a stable income and that you have found a low risk investment.

In order to make your first investment in real estate as simple as possible, it is prudent to look for a property that will *pay for itself*. That means the tenant's rent covers all the costs of the property including the mortgage, rates, insurance, management fees and maintenance. This makes it a *Positive Cash Flow Property*.

If an area has a high occupancy rate, tenants want to live there and the chances of renting the property are high, *as long as the rent is reasonable*. If the occupancy rates are low, you may not be able to find tenants no matter how good the property.

Property management is a job that takes time and effort and is best left in the hands of professionals. Finding a good tenant, attending maintenance issues and collecting rent are tasks you should be willing to pay someone else to do, in order for your investment in real estate to be *passive*.

If you are interested in learning about real estate, there are some great sources of information on the Internet at:

www.realestate.com.au   **www.propertyinvesting.com**   **www.propertyvalue.com.au**

An Opportunity

You have a great opportunity when you are young to make the most of your greatest asset – time. The sooner you find out about the opportunities around you such as owning positive cash flow property, the sooner you can have your first property paid off. Investment in property can be suited to University students as long as it is well managed and doesn't require a lot of effort.

Before buying any real estate:

- Speak to professionals in the field of financial planning, banking, law and real estate.

- Think about why you want to buy it. Will you need to borrow money later on in life?

- Find out what properties are available for sale. What are the prices of houses or units that average working people would rent?

- Find out what properties are available for rent and what the occupancy rates are in different areas. An occupancy rate is the number of houses that are rented divided by the total number of rented plus vacant houses up for rent, as a percentage.

- Find out what *all* the costs of owning a property are. Don't avoid any costs in your calculations and always include figures for general maintenance and rental management.

- Find out what interest rates are for housing and whether they are going up or down. Always factor in at least a 2% increase to any calculations you make.

- Do some calculations and work out if any properties in your area are positive cash flow properties – Would the rent more than pay for all the costs of owning the property? Check that the property you found doesn't need lots of work done to it.

- Start a savings plan and see how you go saving money for a deposit. If you find you can't save money for more than a couple of months, then investing in real estate is probably not for you.

- Go to your bank to find out what sort of money you could borrow with your deposit. Take the figures you have worked out on paper for a typical property.

- Talk to someone in detail, who is already investing in property, to find out all the pros and cons of this type of investing.

- Consider investing in a property trust where your initial investment can be much lower, your risks are spread across a diverse number of properties and someone else has the job of managing your portfolio.

If you decide to enter the property market, always speak to an accountant, a financial advisor, a lawyer and anyone else willing to give you investment advice first. *Never sign anything* until you have spoken to your bank *and they have given you a loan approval*. There is risk involved in any type of investment so find out about and minimise every risk you can. Read books about real estate and other forms of investments. Be realistic and never rush. Investment in real estate can be a great long-term investment plan if all the research is done beforehand and wise decisions are made. It can also be a lot of fun!

Summary

- *Investment in real estate can lead to passive income over time*
- *Banks will generally lend more against average, positive cash flow property*
- *The rent from a positive cash flow property pays for all property costs*

Networking

Networking is about surrounding yourself with people who can help you get to where you want to go. As a University student, your networking group may be your lecturers, work experience mentors and other students around you. Be proud to tell them about what it is you are doing and where you would like to go in the future. I am still working with someone who gave me work experience while I was a student at University over ten years ago. I stay in touch with old friends and occasionally see my lecturers at conferences. That is networking.

It is always good to get to know the key people in your industry, the ones who have either been in their careers for a long time or who intend to stay there. You can learn a lot from them. Successful people often try to learn from others who have done what they want to do. Learning strategies from these people directly is the quickest and most robust way to learn, as they will often tell you what mistakes they made along the way, which allows you the opportunity not to repeat them.

In order to meet people who can guide you with your career and tell you how they became successful, you need to learn how to network. There are many different types of networking – some are formal and some informal, some cost money and some are free. Depending on the type of person you want to learn from and what you want to learn, you could find yourself networking anywhere from formal conferences to a chat over a round of golf.

Networking is all about meeting people with similar interests, goals or experience. You share information, learn from each other and enjoy yourself, all at the same time. A lot of business networking is done on golf courses around the world, as it is a leisurely past time where meeting opponents and chatting is all part of the sport. Be prepared for the people you network with to try to learn something from you too - it's all part of the game.

It's amazing how meeting people often leads to meeting other people and so on and so on. How many times have you done something because of a friend of a friend of a friend? If you go into business, you can set up a group of professionals around you including an accountant, a lawyer, a bank manager, and a business consultant. These people will be crucial to the success of your business and must be kept up-to-date with what you are doing and what you aspire to do in the future.

When the time comes to part company with someone in your network, try to do so only on good terms. Likewise, try to leave a job on good terms with your employer and co-workers, no matter what the reason for your departure.

A bridge burnt through stubbornness or ego is one that may have led to many opportunities.

It is very unprofessional to burn bridges with people in your industry by storming out over a crossed word or a personality clash. You never know when or how that departure may affect you in the future. It is more professional to accept differences, no matter what the grievance, and walk away on talking terms. Agree to disagree and move forward with your head up high. Bridges can always be rebuilt if they haven't been burnt, and networking is all about building bridges to opportunities.

Summary

- *Networking is a way of sharing information in a pleasurable environment*
- *People network at both formal and informal meetings*
- *Staying on good professional terms with colleagues keeps opportunities open*

Invest in Yourself

Investing in yourself is about spending time and perhaps money on your future. Many people avoid thinking about their future because they like to 'have' and 'do' things now, rather than wait until a later point in time. It is always more difficult to concentrate on and invest in the future because by investing, you are sacrificing now for a benefit later on.

Studying a course at University is a good example of investing in yourself. By spending the time, effort and money to go to University, you are setting yourself up for a career in the future, which should bring you better job prospects, more fulfilment and more opportunities. You are sacrificing the opportunity to earn a full-time wage or start a business, in order to learn the skills required to become a professional in your chosen field. This is investing in your education and that approach should never stop, even well after you graduate.

Once you graduate from University, your learning should continue as no degree can teach you everything about a topic. It is just an introduction to a career that allows you to work in the profession. Don't ever fool yourself by thinking that having a degree makes you an expert in that profession. Expertise comes after many years of dedication, working, researching, continually improving and discovering.

Attending Conferences

There will be many opportunities after you graduate to update your knowledge and skills by listening to experts in your field at refresher courses, exhibitions, conferences and discussions, which may be available in person or on the Internet. Absorb as much as possible at these functions. Be choosy about which ones you attend as there are plenty of people making money out of setting up conferences. Make sure you attend only those that are of benefit and interest to you and provide value for money.

If you become involved in an area of research or discover something new from the work you do, you may have the opportunity to speak at conferences or take out a patent of your own. By doing this, you will be putting yourself and your name forward as a contributor to the knowledge bank of your profession. If your information provides your peers with new, reliable knowledge, your efforts should be well received.

Keep investing in yourself and make the effort to stay up-to-date with the information and technology of your chosen career. Look for interesting opportunities to network and spend time each year taking your knowledge forward. Avoid only holding on to what you learn at University, as technology and information is changing all the time. By staying open to new ideas and continuing to learn, you will avoid becoming a professional dinosaur!

Summary

● *Studying for a degree at University is a great investment in yourself*

● *Continue to invest in your education even after you graduate*

● *Attending and contributing to conferences will keep your knowledge up-to-date*

Dealing with Success and Failure

Personal Responsibility

Be *personally responsible* for your own successes and failures. Try to accept and admit your weaknesses if you find yourself struggling. There is plenty of help available to anyone who takes responsibility for their own inadequacies. Equally, be prepared to accept a compliment graciously if your classmate or lecturer congratulates you for an achievement.

"Success is the ability to go from one failure to another with no loss of enthusiasm"
Sir Winston Churchill (1874 - 1965)

Some students blame anyone and everyone for their failures and very few people have any patience for these students. A 'bad' lecturer or tutor is usually blamed. Accept that your lecturers' and tutors' abilities add an insignificant margin to your success in any one subject. The bulk of the effort is up to you. Only you can do the research and read the books. Only you can sit the exams. If you feel that a lecturer or tutor is letting you down with substandard notes or information, then question them until a satisfactory outcome is reached. No examination board will accept that you failed a subject because your lecturer was no good, if you hadn't brought it to their attention well before the exam.

Self Reliance

A lecturer is there to guide you. Don't rely on them to give you everything you need for a test or exam. If you are in any doubt, look at past exam papers and find out for yourself what you need to learn for a subject. If you don't think you are learning all you need, ask a lot of questions and if you're still not happy with the answers, ask someone else who has the ability to steer you in the right direction.

Plagiarism

There are *cheating syndicates* in Universities and of course there is no merit in what these groups do - they usually get found out sooner or later. Other students choose to plagiarise via the Internet or copy out of books. These students also get caught, as there are sophisticated suites of software that can check the uniqueness of a piece of writing. It is common practice for all assignments to be checked for plagiarism. Be prepared to take full responsibility if you are caught and don't be fooled to think that if you are part of a guilty group, you will be punished less severely. Students have ruined their careers by being exposed as a cheat at University. Don't let this happen to you.

Envy

Being successful can in itself bring you grief if your friends or family become envious. You will know whom your true friends are when they stick by you whether you are successful or not. Some people prefer everyone to stay at the same level, and feel uncomfortable if someone they know becomes more successful than they are. I have seen this myself at University as well as in my working career.

Although it is very sad, it is a natural reaction for these people and there is not a lot that can be done about it. Bringing it out into to the open by trying to talk to them can often make it worse as they very rarely admit the real reason they are offended. To avoid becoming embroiled in their nastiness, it is often better to break contact with them. Stopping yourself from succeeding to please someone else makes no sense at all.

Generosity

Always remember that your success is not all about you. Most people succeed by helping other people solve a problem. If you do become successful, the best way for you to use that success is to give it back to others. There may be nothing more satisfying than being able to share the freedom you enjoy from your own success.

Summary

- *Be personally responsible for your successes and failures*
- *Avoid plagiarism at all costs as it will catch up with you in time*
- *Be wary of envy within yourself and others and strive for generosity instead*

Postgraduate Study

Decide for Yourself

Postgraduate study can lead to qualifications beyond a Bachelor's Degree. It usually leads to a Masters Degree or Doctorate of Philosophy (PhD). This type of study requires the student to perform unique research on a subject that brings new results or teachings to their field. When someone has a Masters Degree or PhD, they are very knowledgeable about a specific topic and they have proven to the examiners that they have the ability to do independent research.

If you have the desire to undertake postgraduate studies, weigh up the pros and cons of doing the extra work before you commit to it. The work involved in doing postgraduate studies is immense and because you have to work on a unique topic, you will be creating the research yourself. It's not like studying for an undergraduate degree where you take classes and study for exams. During a postgraduate course, you are setting up the experiments, doing the surveys and hypothesising about why things are the way they are. No one is telling you what to learn, you have to work it out for yourself.

With that sort of commitment, you need to have just as much passion, if not more, as you did in your undergraduate course. Without passion, your postgraduate degree would become a chore which makes it difficult to think uniquely and generate new ideas. You need to be searching for a solution to a problem or wanting to find out why something happens like it does. Only then might you have the inner capacity to achieve what postgraduate study is designed for.

> When I was finishing my undergraduate degree, I was lured into starting my Masters Degree, with a vision of continuing on to do a PhD. At the time, I considered a PhD to be the pinnacle of University study and my ego was flattered at the prospect of being offered a scholarship. When I enrolled to start, I was given a choice of two topics to study – neither of which I found interesting. I had no passion. I was essentially being asked to study a topic that someone else had a passion for but it wasn't my passion. I lacked direction and the desire to get stuck into my research and ended up quitting after 4 months. I was so glad when I did finish, as the topic I chose was just not for me.

If you want to do well at Postgraduate study, make sure you are passionate about what you are going to research. Don't feel you have to continue straight on from your Bachelor's Degree. If you are offered a scholarship, find out what your options are first before you make your decision and weigh up whether you think it might be better if you got some experience working in the field before you commit to a topic. After all, how can you know where your passions lie in your chosen career if you haven't worked in it yet?

Having a *postgraduate degree* is certainly a great asset if you want to work in the world of academia or in a research field. However, be careful not to over qualify yourself if you want to work in a practical career where a postgraduate degree is not required. In my working career, I have seen many postgraduate degree holders miss out on jobs *because they had a PhD*. Consider a postgraduate degree if you have a strong passion for finding out why or how something works, not because someone else wants you to find it out for them. Think about proposing your topic to the University rather than letting them give you topics to choose from. There is generally no age limit for performing postgraduate work, so you should be able to come back at any stage when you find out for yourself where your passions lie.

Summary

- *Postgraduate study is suitable for those wanting to do their own research*
- *A Postgraduate degree is a great asset although not necessary for all careers*
- *Being passionate about what you study will help keep you motivated*

Deferring

When you defer from your studies, you take time off to pursue something else before going back to University. You may want to work for a year, travel or take time off to help a sick relative. There may be an exchange program between your University and another that you'd like to take part in or you may be offered work in another country. Deferring is common, although not all Universities automatically hold your position, so it is important to discuss your plans with them well before you leave.

After saving up in my final year of High School and planning my trip overseas, I was surprised to find out that the Veterinary course I was admitted to would not hold my place if I deferred for a year. I decided to go anyway because they assured me that I would get in again if I just re-applied when I returned.

Personal Growth through Travel - Some students yearn to travel while they have the opportunity before starting a family or full-time employment. There are many different opinions about whether or not it is a good thing for a student to do. Those who have travelled themselves usually believe that travel is a positive experience that broadens the mind and enriches the student's potential. Others who have not travelled often worry that taking a year off during a University degree would be a negative experience and one that may result in the student not ever coming back to finish their degree.

If you have the urge to go somewhere, travelling or taking a gap year during your University course can be a great thing! The life skills learnt while away can be truly wonderful and give you fond memories to cherish for many years. It can also broaden your horizons with respect to future employment, as you may meet lots of people while you are away. If on the other hand you have no urge to go anywhere, it may be just as good for you not to travel and make similar connections with people from your own country.

For some students, the thought of travelling overseas is a very daunting prospect. For others, it is an exciting challenge. Therefore, travelling while a student is not going to be good for everyone. Some may want to travel alone while others may want to travel with friends. As long as you do not feel *forced* to travel with or without someone you need or want, things can run smoothly. Don't ever feel pressured to travel somewhere with a friend if you are not fully in favour of going. Friendships can be ruined in this way.

Planning is a crucial key to a successful trip, especially if more than one person is involved. On your own, it is a lot easier to change plans on a whim. When someone else is with you, it is important to consider his or her objectives as well as your own, or the trip can quickly turn ugly.

When deciding whether or not to go away for an extended period of time as a University student, it is important to consider the consequences and weigh them up along with the benefits. Usually, your urge to travel drives you to earn the extra money needed to pay for the trip. You may have to convince your family, friends and lecturers that your plans will be a positive thing for you. You may be confronted with some suggesting it is a bad idea. But if you are totally prepared and ready to go, you may just be able to change their mind.

I had an enormous urge to travel the year after I finished High School. That year had been particularly stressful and I felt I needed the total break away from studying in order to have a fresh mind to begin University. In the typical Australian backpacker fashion, I took the following year off studies to travel around the world. I earned the money I needed by baby-sitting, working in fast food outlets and picking grapes and took great pride in organising everything on my own. I had a wonderful year away visiting Africa, Europe and Canada and by the time I returned, I was refreshed and ready for University. Had I not gone away,

I'm sure I would have felt burnt out and stale, even in my first year. I travelled alone and just loved the freedom that allowed me. I was so lucky to have the support of my friends and family who were all very encouraging and showed interest in what I was doing.

Insurance

Travel insurance is a very important consideration if you decide to go overseas, especially if you go to a country with very expensive medical costs or where crime rates are high. Protection of your passport is also crucial, as you don't want to end up stranded without one. Always store your passport in a safe place and keep photocopies of the personal information page in different parts of your luggage. Taking travellers' cheques or using a credit card instead of holding lots of cash is another consideration. Cash is a very desirable commodity that has no protection if it is stolen. Travellers' cheques and credit cards at least offer some sort of protection.

Emergencies

The 112 GSM International Standard Emergency Access Number allows you to be connected to a local emergency number *anywhere in the world* (where GSM network coverage is available) by dialling 112 from your mobile phone (even if your keypad is locked or SIM card is not present in the phone). Calling 112 is just like calling a local emergency number. It is a *FREE* call.

By dialling 112 you can contact the following emergency services:

- Ambulance Services

- Police Services

- Fire Services

The 112 GSM International Standard Emergency Access Number is automatically activated, free of charge, when you connect your mobile service. For more information go to:

www.emergencycalls.aca.gov.au

Foreign Laws

Understanding and abiding by the *laws* of countries you visit is important for every traveller. There is no excuse for not knowing local laws as a tourist and for that reason it is very wise to read about the countries you want to visit, well before you travel.

Immunisation

Immunisation for disease is a very important protection for yourself while you are away. Most foreign diseases can be avoided by taking a simple precaution before you leave. Make sure you give your body the correct amount of time for any vaccination to take effect before you enter the country. Again, there is no excuse for not knowing what precautions you should take, as this information is readily available at any reputable medical clinic, travel agent or consulate.

If you do decide to defer and you accept that you will come back a year behind your peers at University, then try to enjoy yourself and make full use of the time away, to see the places you want to see and experience life away from studying. Don't go travelling and then spend all your time away worrying about the consequences. Accept the consequences and move on.

While I was tutoring High School students who wanted to travel, I was often asked by one or both of the student's parents whether I thought it was a good idea or not. My answer was always that the travel experience would be good if there was a strong desire from the student to go. It had to be planned well and enough money had to be saved for the student to survive and do some of the things they wanted to do. There is no point travelling if you don't have enough money to enjoy the experience.

Most parents were worried that their child would not come back to University if they deferred after High School. I always used myself as an example of a student who was pretty tired after High School and needed a break from studying in order to re-focus. I came back from my travels a lot wiser and with a different perspective on life, which allowed me to concentrate more on my studies at University. I didn't feel like a perpetual student and had learned what life was like out in the big world.

Now that I am a parent myself however, I can understand some of the concerns other parents have and that is just something they have to discuss with the student well in advance of organising any trip. For me, it had been a great experience and continues to give me many fond memories. I would never begrudge anyone that sense of adventure and freedom and the opportunity to experience all that travelling has to offer.

Travel is great for those who seek to experience new countries and their cultures. For those who don't have a burning desire, it may be better for them to stay put and work on the dreams they do have. Therefore travel is neither necessary for success nor a guarantee of success. Students should weigh up the pros and cons and decide for themselves. There is no right or wrong answer here. The urge to travel may not be there one year and yet be very strong another year. This is normal. I find I get the travel bug every two to three years. I have some friends however who have never had the urge to travel and they are quite happy to stay where they are.

The consequence, that you start a University course a year later because you go travelling, is not a huge negative that should stop you going altogether. It is a consequence that may in the long run be beneficial for you. Some students are immature and not really ready for University when they go straight from High School. A year away certainly allows a student to mature and in many cases, they become more focused on what they really want to do when they have quality time to think about it.

When I was a High School student, all I wanted to do was be a vet. I was so sure that I was going to be a vet that I didn't look at any other profession when I applied to go to veterinary school. When I got into the veterinary course at University, I told them that I had planned to take a year off to travel and I would like to start the following year. My urge to travel was so strong that within a couple of months, I was off travelling the world.

While I was away and had plenty of time to think, it dawned on me that I hadn't looked at any other profession. I spent a lot of time thinking about being a vet and even went to see some vets in London to talk to them about what it was really like. To my great surprise, I found that it wasn't what I really wanted to do after all, even though I really loved animals. I was able then to spend time researching different professions and finally came up with Engineering as something I was really interested in. I am now a practising engineer and I really love my work. Had it not been for my trip away and the opportunity to scrutinise my direction, I may well have become a very frustrated vet!

If you do decide to travel while you are a student, be sure to look up the STA Travel website or pop into one of their branches. When I was at University, there was a branch at my campus and they were able to help me organise a lot of things like air fares, Eurail tickets (railway tickets for travelling in Europe), Heritage passes (to see fantastic historic sites around the UK) and they also introduced me to Youth Hostelling. There are amazing discounts for travelling students, so make sure you find out about them well before you travel.

Check out these websites before you spend any money on your travels:

STA Travel – Discount Student Travel

www.sta.com

YHA Australia – Worldwide Discount Accommodation

www.yha.com.au

International SOS - Worldwide Emergency Assistance

www.internationalsos.com

Spend some time writing down the answers to these questions before you make any decisions about taking a year off University to travel. You should find some direction in the answers you provide.

My urge to travel is: a. Very Strong   b. Strong   c. Neutral   d. Non-existent

If I travelled, I would go to: _____

If I travelled, I would go: a. By myself

                                     b. With _____

                                     who has a compatible personality and similar travelling aims.

If I travelled, it would cost: _____

If I travelled, the consequences to my University degree would be _____

_____

_____

Summary

- *If you decide to defer, discuss your intentions with your University*
- *You can defer for any number of reasons – medical, travel, work or exchange*
- *Deferring may offer the break you need to re-focus your studies*

Work Readiness

As a final chapter to *University Wisdom*, I discuss the importance of being ready for job interviews or starting a business after you graduate. These first steps outside the campus into the business world can be daunting, but with enough preparation the transition should be smooth. It is important to be prepared for this moment, as it will be with you sooner than you imagine.

So how will you know when you are ready to *leave University* and take on your first job in your career? Hopefully your course is accredited, which means it fulfils the requirements set out by the governing bodies in your profession. This is the responsibility of your University. Always check this out, especially if you are doing an online degree. Find out whether it is accredited in the country you want to work in. If it is accredited and you graduate with your degree after passing the minimum number of required subjects, you should by default, have as much understanding about the job as a *graduate in the field is expected to have*.

A graduate position is generally a junior position in most fields, so you will not be expected to be an 'expert' as soon as you finish your degree. A common misconception students have is that they will be an expert as soon as they get their degree. Experience in your field and working for many years is equivalent to studying for many degrees. No one becomes a true expert without being a graduate first and slowly but surely finding their niche.

There are no guarantees that you will even get a job in your chosen career straight away. Don't expect that your degree or your marks will guarantee you a high paying job. Graduate positions are generally not highly paid. When there are more students finishing a course than the number of jobs available, it is inevitable that some graduates will have to look at a career change or at the very least, the possibility of working in another state or country. These eventualities should lead to a feeling of challenge and excitement, rather than disappointment. Any change can be made into a positive experience if seen through the right perspective.

When you go for your *interviews*, make sure you don't focus too much on your course and your marks. By the time someone decides to interview you, they have already assumed that you have fulfilled the academic requirements of your degree. You don't need to dwell on subjects or marks, ranking or details. What your interviewer is trying to do is find out whether or not you are a nice person, what your attitude to working is and whether you'll be a good person to work with. They will want to know whether you have a sense of humour, an interesting outlook on life and a unique personality.

Your interviewer may ask if you have any questions. You don't have to necessarily think of a clever question - you can simply ask them what sort of work they do personally and how they enjoy working for the company. This sort of response can get both people talking as potential colleagues.

When you get *your first job*, try to establish a mentoring relationship with someone who would know what you are expected to be learning. There doesn't need to be a formal mentoring program but you should be able to ask this person for advice when you need to.

A mentoring relationship needs to be open, honest and a two-way channel. Be choosy when you set this up as some people may be happy to act as a mentor and some may not. You need to get to know the people you work with before you decide who the best person might be. Personality and politics can play an interesting role, just keep the relationship simple and be grateful for any help your mentor gives you. Try to be prepared for meetings you have with them and be mindful that they will have many commitments and time constraints placed on them in their own role.

Your first job as a graduate may be short-term or could last your whole career. Either way, it is another very exciting stepping-stone in your life and career. Be challenged by all you are given to do but more importantly, tuck all you learn away in your 'tool box' for the next chapter in your career. You never know where your first job or the contacts you meet there may lead you.

Summary

- *An accredited University degree makes you ready for a graduate position*
- *An interviewer will be looking at your personal qualities and attitudes*
- *Try to find a mentoring figure at your first job to guide you*

Summaries

This list brings together all the summaries from each chapter as a quick reference.

Chapter 1 - Congratulations
- *Acknowledge the hard work you have done to get you where you are now*
- *Be grateful to all the people who have helped you along the way*
- *Think of your degree at University as a stepping-stone to your career*

Chapter 2 – What is University?
- *University is a place where people learn new skills*
- *There are many different courses and institutions around the world*
- *Obtaining a University degree is both challenging and rewarding*

Chapter 3 – Discover Your Influences
- *Your decision to go to University should be clearly understood*
- *Take responsibility for your decision to go to University*
- *Having a positive attitude towards your course is the first step towards success*

Chapter 4 – Is University For You?
- *Not everyone is convinced that they will enjoy University before they start*
- *There are always solutions to problems faced by students*
- *Try to control the amount of stress you place on yourself*

Chapter 5 – Define Success For You
- *Your success should only be determined by your own definitions*
- *There are at least five areas of success to strive for*
- *When you reach your own definition of success – be happy!*

Chapter 6 – Choosing a Course
- *There may be many careers that you are suited to and would be happy in*
- *Your decision now is not going to 'lock you in' for life*
- *Get to know yourself, as it will help you in your course choice*

Chapter 7 – Plan for Success
- *A plan is a list of goals with time frames*
- *Any large goal can be broken down into achievable steps*
- *Being organised with a plan makes it easier to achieve goals*

Chapter 8 – Be Inspired
- *An inspiration can help you focus on achieving your goals*
- *An inspiration that comes from within you is most powerful*
- *A visual reminder of your goal and inspiration will help cement it in your mind*

Chapter 9 - Think Beyond Your Marks
- *Avoid putting excessive pressure on yourself – keep your marks in perspective*
- *Talk to the people who care for you when you feel disappointed*
- *You can't change your mistakes so learn from them!*

Chapter 10 – Body Care
- *Caring for your body is an essential part of achieving and enjoying success*
- *Body care involves regular exercise, proper posture, a healthy diet and sleep*
- *Caring for your body can help keep you motivated*

Chapter 11 – Smoking, Drugs and Alcohol
- *Be choosy about the people you spend your time with*
- *It's OK to say 'No'*
- *Never give in to peer group pressure – Have confidence to say what you mean*

Chapter 12 – University Clubs and Facilities
- *University clubs and facilities are there for your use*
- *Join clubs that you have time for and will enjoy becoming involved in*
- *Some Universities have reciprocal rights with others around the world*

Chapter 13 – Image Protection
- *A first impression is hard to change*
- *Be the person you want to be every day – 'What comes around, goes around'*
- *Be polite and stay honest – you never know who you'll bump into later on*

Chapter 14 – What to Wear
- *Wear clothes that are comfortable*
- *Make sure your shoes are sturdy and will endure high usage*
- *Keep a sweater on campus in case you need it*

Chapter 15 – Financial Budget
- *Understand what you spend your money on*
- *Decide whether or not your are living within your means*
- *Complete a financial budget, stick to it and review it regularly*

Chapter 16 – Choosing Subjects
- *Find out which subjects are compulsory and which are elective*
- *You need more than the incentive of money to do well in a career*
- *Mix up a variety of subjects to make your course balanced and interesting*

Chapter 17 – Mutual Respect
- *Use your mind in a positive way - 'Don't look down' on others*
- *Keep a healthy respect for yourself and for others around you*
- *Share your knowledge to experience the benefits of your own generosity*

Chapter 18 – Time Management
- *There are many tools available to help you manage your time*
- *Students need to use time management skills to win the race against time*
- *Always leave time to review assignments before you hand them in*

Chapter 19 – Using a Diary
- *A diary allows you to plan your assignments, commitments and entertainment*
- *Use a tick next to any accomplished tasks in your diary*
- *Keep your diary with you - then you can write things down as they happen*

Chapter 20 – 80% and 2-Day Rule®
- *The 80% and 2-Day Rule® allows you to plan assignments using your diary*
- *Use 80% of the given time to do your assignment*
- *Review your assignment and print it out at least 2 days before it is due*

Chapter 21 – Goal Setting
- *Use a 'to do' list to organise and prioritise your goals*
- *Use a 'don't list' to commit to giving up habits you shouldn't have*
- *Break down complex goals into a series of achievable ones*

Chapter 22 – Focus
- *Separate your assignments into discrete, manageable tasks*
- *Use a clear workspace for each task so you can focus on them one at a time*
- *Free up your time by working efficiently and effectively*

Chapter 23 – Time Line
- *A time line gives you a window into your future*
- *Your goals can be changed at any time depending on your circumstances*
- *Look forward to achieving the goals you set yourself!*

Chapter 24 – Form Good Habits
- *There are good habits and bad habits*
- *Only good habits can take you closer to wherever it is you want to go*
- *Eliminating bad habits can help you get there faster*

Chapter 25 – Communicate and Act Promptly
- *Acknowledge confusion or the need for review when it happens*
- *Seek out the appropriate help*
- *Control your problems so they don't control you*

Chapter 26 – Learn from Others
- *Listen to other students' questions and the answers they are given*
- *Learn to read signals from your lecturer when they highlight important points*
- *Avoid copying at all costs – it will always catch up with you*

Chapter 27 – Using a Computer
- *A computer can make your work and research at University more efficient*
- *Save your work regularly to a removable backup device*
- *Good computer skills is an advantage at University as well as in the work force*

Chapter 28 – Using the Internet
- *The Internet is an easily accessible tool containing vast amounts of information*
- *Information found on the Internet should always be verified*
- *Use a security system to protect your computer and keep it updated*

Chapter 29 – Have an Outlet
- *Choose an outlet that refreshes your mind and body*
- *Make time to attend your outlet on a weekly basis*
- *Use your outlet as a reward when you complete goals*

Chapter 30 – Student Loans

- *Always understand the terms and conditions of any loan you agree to*
- *Make sure you will be able to meet your loan repayments comfortably*
- *Extra payments can reduce your loan term – always check for any penalties*

Chapter 31 – Scholarships

- *There are thousands of scholarships offered to students all over the world*
- *You need to find a scholarship whose criteria you meet*
- *Make sure you apply for scholarships by the due date in order to be considered*

Chapter 32 – Getting Experience

- *Having work experiences as a student will give you insight into different careers*
- *Work experience is just that – The pay is a bonus*
- *Your Resume will draw on all your experiences – Make the most of them*

Chapter 33 – Life's Limitations

- *We are all limited by time and money*
- *Try to use what you have to its full potential by making wise decisions*
- *Reducing what you spend in one area allows you to spend more in another*

Chapter 34 – Accept Sacrifices

- *Short-term sacrifices may have to be made while you are a student*
- *The benefits of a good career choice far outweigh the sacrifices*
- *Enjoy the unique lifestyle and benefits of being a student while you can*

Chapter 35 – The Roller Coaster

- *There are pros and cons of every course and every career*
- *Some problems stem from the mind, while others are beyond your control*
- *Visualising yourself dealing with problems helps you to prepare for them*

Chapter 36 – Workers and Surfers vs Balance

- *Workers and Surfers often make life hard for themselves unnecessarily*
- *Try to find and maintain balance as a University student*
- *Do your best with the talent, resources and support you have*

Chapter 37 – Exam Technique

- *Write clear, readable, correct and complete answers*
- *Use visualisation as a tool for memorising information*
- *Once you have the knowledge, use past exams to hone your speed and timing*

Chapter 38 – Earning Money

- *A part-time job while studying can be very rewarding*
- *Be wary of the number of hours you work and travel during the week*
- *Try to find a job that is enjoyable for you and has flexible working hours*

Chapter 39 – Politics and Charities

- *Politics can be a good platform for public speaking and debating*
- *Consider your main aim when deciding whether or not to get involved*
- *There are many groups already working around the world that you can support*

Chapter 40 – Relationships
- *Relationships should be mutually beneficial and enjoyable for both partners*
- *Talking to your partner can usually solve any problems that arise*
- *Consider your primary aim when dealing with a 'difficult' relationship*

Chapter 41 – Follow Your Plan
- *Each strategy you adopt may require an extra effort of 5%*
- *Having a plan and following it will lead to your goals being achieved*
- *Using more than one strategy in your plan may create a compounding effect*

Chapter 42 – Investing Money
- *Investment and saving takes time and commitment*
- *Compounding allows interest or benefits to accumulate*
- *A good Credit Rating is a valuable asset – Protect yours*

Chapter 43 – Positive Cash Flow Property
- *Investment in real estate can lead to passive income over time*
- *Banks will generally lend more against average, positive cash flow property*
- *The rent from a positive cash flow property pays for all property costs*

Chapter 44 – Networking
- *Networking is a way of sharing information in a pleasurable environment*
- *People network at both formal and informal meetings*
- *Staying on good professional terms with colleagues keeps opportunities open*

Chapter 45 – Invest in Yourself
- *Studying for a degree at University is a great investment in yourself*
- *Continue to invest in your education even after you graduate*
- *Attending and contributing to conferences will keep your knowledge up-to-date*

Chapter 46 – Dealing with Success and Failure
- *Be personally responsible for your successes and failures*
- *Avoid plagiarism at all costs as it will catch up with you in time*
- *Be wary of envy within yourself and others and strive for generosity instead*

Chapter 47 – Post Graduate Study
- *Postgraduate study is suitable for those wanting to do their own research*
- *A Postgraduate degree is a great asset although not necessary for all careers*
- *Being passionate about what you study will help keep you motivated*

Chapter 48 – Deferring
- *If you decide to defer, discuss your intentions with your University*
- *You can defer for any number of reasons – medical, travel, work, exchange*
- *Deferring may offer the break you need to re-focus your studies*

Chapter 49 – Work Readiness
- *An accredited University degree makes you ready for a graduate position*
- *An interviewer will be looking at your personal qualities and attitudes*
- *Try to find a mentoring figure at your first job to guide you*

A Message to the Reader _____

Thank you for taking the time to read through *University Wisdom*. I hope you have enjoyed it and have gained some practical strategies to help you through your University experience. I wish you well on your journey and invite you to send me your feedback about the book or about the strategies you try. Please send your comments to me by email at

feedback@universitywisdom.com

After leaving High School in 1987, until I finished my University degrees in 1995, I tutored students in their final years of High School. This was a part-time job for me while I was studying at University. My aim originally was for the tutoring to pay for my transport costs. Yet I always found it difficult to say no to a new student who needed help. So at the height of my tutoring I was helping 15 students every week while studying full-time for a double degree.

I found tutoring very satisfying but was frustrated that I couldn't help more students. Ninety percent of those I taught were keen to learn and it gave me great pleasure seeing them understand a concept. Their grateful smiles and sighs of relief made me feel good about what I was doing. I was interested in how they were coping, how they did in their exams and then what they decided to do with themselves beyond their High School years. I still occasionally get phone calls from those students now and I delight in sharing their achievements.

Apart from the obvious questions students asked me relating to their subject, there was another set of questions that surfaced year after year. They were curious about how they were going to change from High School students to full-time University students and then, ultimately, to successful working professionals. They were concerned about going to University, wondered what it was like, how they were going to cope with the pressures and how they would have the skills to complete their degree and get a 'good job'. Most of my students' parents had never gone to University, so they were unable to give them the advice they were looking for.

**The questions my High School students have asked me about University
form the basis of this book.**

My aim for *University Wisdom* is for it to be an easy-to-read guide, giving students like you access to some powerful knowledge and tools for success. I set out to create a book that could be read within a week. I wanted it to be thought provoking and mentally expanding. The simple exercises in this book should have unlocked some of your inner thoughts, which may otherwise have been kept in your subconscious for your entire life.

Having some knowledge before it is needed is always better than learning from your mistakes, as by then it may be too late. This book gives you some knowledge up front, so you don't have to wait around for years to learn through your own experiences.

Hopefully now, you can embark on the great adventure of University with confidence. Give yourself the best chance of making it a successful, balanced and happy experience. The strategies you learn by reading *University Wisdom* may help your journey have focus and direction, leading to a better outcome for your life and your career.

When the font changes to this hand writing style, I talk about my own personal experiences while at University. I explain how I was feeling at the time and how I coped with what was expected of me. I was once, just like you.

This book was not intended to be an exhaustive description of what to do and what not to do with your life. That would be an impossible task and make any book terribly boring to read. Individuals are different and each needs to be able to draw out the relevant information to make them more positive and ready to face life's challenges.

You may find that you want to refer to this book during your course when you need to re-focus your thoughts. When we get totally involved in something like a University degree, it is sometimes difficult to find the time to think of anything else. This book and its exercises are presented in a very simple to understand format, so using the book as a future reference can be easy. You will not have to reread the whole book in order to understand each chapter. You will probably be amused as you look back on your initial answers to the exercises.

As you grow as an individual and have the interaction of others studying at University to shape your life experiences, the answers to the exercises in this book may change. Capturing these changes in black and white will be fascinating, so make sure you write them down each time you read through the chapters.

Think clearly about what you read; listen to others and then make your own decisions. Don't ever follow anyone's advice blindly. As time goes by and your situation changes, your set of ideas and strategies may also need to change. Keep an open mind and always weigh up each and every suggestion on its own merits.

Lack of education and poverty are both great contributors to crime and suffering in the world. Acknowledgement of this along with a dose of generosity from the educated few is the only way that things can improve. Using your education to help others help themselves is one way of contributing to the balance in life. It is one of my many reasons for writing this book.

I hope you enjoyed reading *University Wisdom* and have gained some really useful ideas from it. Remember however, that ideas are just ideas until you put them to work.

Good Luck with your journey

Vanessa McCallum

About the Author

Vanessa McCallum began her University degrees in 1990 after travelling the world for 12 months at age 18. She studied Science and Engineering at Monash University in Clayton, Melbourne Australia. While Vanessa was at University she tutored High School students in Maths and Science. Her experiences with her students led to her desire to help other students, which culminated in the writing of this book.

Vanessa's studies at University were enhanced by a six-month working opportunity in Switzerland with ABB (Asea Brown Boveri). This was a great experience allowing her to network with other students from all over the world. She also took the opportunity to realise one of her life-long goals of climbing the Matterhorn. These positive experiences have enriched Vanessa's horizons enough for her to want others to achieve their goals as well.

Vanessa is now at a stage in her life where she is building businesses and creating passive income so she is less reliant on her formal job. This will free up her time to work on her own projects and spend more time with her family. Her ultimate goal is to help others find this freedom. This book is her first attempt to help students organise and balance their lives, so that their success and eventual freedom is possible.

Please send any comments regarding this book to feedback@universitywisdom.com

Glossary

Some of the terms used in this book may require a little explanation....

0-10

80% and 2-Day Rule®

A method of ensuring you finish your assignments on time and physically have them ready for submission on or before the due date.

A

Academic Requirements

The core requirements stipulated by the University for a student to pass a degree.

B

Bachelor's Degree

A degree earned by students after they leave High School - usually a prerequisite for beginning a Masters degree or PhD.

Burnout

When a student works very hard without a break. Their performance reduces and they often feel physically and mentally drained resulting in a loss of a desire to continue.

C

Campus

The physical location within the boundaries of the University.

Curriculum Vitae (CV)

A brief summary of your identity as well as the notable achievements and experiences you have gained to date. (Same as Resume).

D

Deferral

When a student takes time off studying at University to pursue something else, like travel, work or an exchange.

Double Degree	When two degrees are studied simultaneously, leading to two separate degrees being obtained by the student. Usually the time taken to finish the two degrees is shorter than if each was taken one at a time.
Dux	The student who achieves the top marks at the end of the academic year.

E

eBook	A book that can be downloaded and printed from the Internet via a computer.
Enrolment Day	A day set aside before the start of first term each year when students organise what subjects they will take.
Examination	A formal test carried out to ascertain the students' understanding of subject matter and to rank the class according to ability.

F

Facilities	Equipment and services that the University provides for students to use for their study, enjoyment, exercise and relaxation.
First Year Student	A student of any age who is in their first year at University. (Same as Fresher)
Fresher	A student of any age who is in their first year at University. (Same as First Year Student)
Full-time	A full-time student studying a degree attends during the week and is expected to dedicate a considerable amount of time to their studies.

G

Graduate	A student who completes and satisfies all the academic requirements of a University degree. The student obtains a certificate from the University stating which degree they have obtained.

H

High School	A place of learning for students before they attend University.

I

Internet A worldwide system of linked computers that allows information exchange.

Institution Any place of learning offering post High School education.

Investment Making a sacrifice in time or money now for a benefit in the future.

J

Job Employment for an individual where money is earned in exchange for work done.

K

Knowledge An understanding of a subject that can be tested or displayed in detail.

L

Landlord A person or company who owns a house or commercial property and rents it out to a tenant.

Listed Company A company whose shares are listed on a stock exchange and can be bought and sold by the public.

M

Main Aim The aim with the highest priority. The main aim of a person is their primary focus.

Mentor A person who guides a student or graduate and gives them the opportunity to ask questions.

N

Network A group of individuals with a common interest who work together to achieve great results.

O

Open Day A day that prospective students can go to University to see what it is like and ask questions about the course they are interested in. Many students usually volunteer to help during Open Days and they may take visitors on tours of the University or offer to help with answering questions.

Orientation Day	This day is usually the first day for First Year students before any formal classes are held. It usually consists of tours of the facilities available to students such as the libraries, sporting facilities and shops.
Outlet	Any activity that takes a students' mind away from their studies, allowing them to come back to study feeling refreshed.

P

Part-time	A part-time student studying a degree who attends a couple of days or nights per week and who is expected to dedicate a moderate amount of time to their studies. A part-time degree usually takes longer to obtain than a full-time degree.
Passion	A hobby or inspiration that pushes a student to perform at a higher level.
Plagiarism	The copying of a piece of work written by another person.

Q

Qualification	The degree or certificate obtained by a student or worker by attending a course. A qualification is not necessarily obtained at a University. Many companies offer qualifications specific to their line of business.

R

Reciprocal Rights	An agreement between Universities where students can gain access to facilities or memberships at other campuses.
Resume	A brief summary of your identity as well as the notable achievements and experiences you have gained to date. (Same as Curriculum Vitae or CV).

S

Scholarship	An offer to a student who fits certain criteria for financial or other help towards their studies. A scholarship can also include the opportunity of work experience and can be made by a group, a private or corporate entity or by a government.
Special Consideration	A student can apply to the examination board of a University for special consideration when they have experienced exceptional circumstances such as illness, family tragedy or any other unavoidable circumstances that affects their ability to perform at examinations.

Student Loan

A loan given to a University Student in order for them to pay for their course or a computer or other item such as a car. The interest rate is generally higher than a mortgage as there is usually very little or no security. Many different institutions offer student loans including banks, Universities and governments.

T

Tenant

A person who signs a contract with the owner of a house or commercial property to rent the property for a period.

Timetable

A regular pattern of classes to be attended, written down in tabular format, including times, places and class descriptions.

U

Undergraduate

A student studying for a degree but who has yet to graduate.

University

An institution offering post High School students accredited courses, leading to certification.

V

Verifiable Source

Information that can be traced back to a credible author or institution, whose information can be relied upon or checked.

W

Website

A file sitting on a computer that can be read by the public over the Internet. Websites can display information or gather information from visitors.

Y

Year Off

When a student defers their studies to travel, work, exchange or take part in any other activity.

References

1: UNESCO Global Education Digest 2004 for Enrolments at University

2: Population Division of the Department of Economic and Social Affairs of the United Nations Secretariat – World Population Prospects : The 2004 Revision Population Database

3: Mean historical return for listed property January 1971 - March 2005 of 14.8%. CCH, Australian Master Financial Planning Guide, 2005/2006, Edition 8, August 2005, Page 426. McPherson's Printing Group, ISBN 1 921022 52 3 Management fees and taxes reduce net earnings to approximately 10% per annum.

4: Information was extracted from various websites for this graph. Rates are indicative only and an average of the values.

Index

DATE DUE

HIGHSMITH 45230